5
Leadership
Essentials
for Women

5

Leadership

Essentials

for Women

Developing Your Ability
to Make Things Happen

COMPILED BY

Linda Clark

new
hope
PUBLISHERS

Birmingham, Alabama

New Hope® Publishers
P. O. Box 12065
Birmingham, AL 35202-2065
www.newhopepublishers.com

Library of Congress Cataloging-in-Publication Data
Clark, Linda, 1944-
5 leadership essentials for women : developing your ability to make
things happen / compiled by Linda Clark.
p. cm.
ISBN 1-56309-842-3 (pbk.)
1. Christian leadership. 2. Women in church work. I. Title: Five leadership essentials for women. II. Title.
BV652.1.C555 2004
248.8'43—dc22
2004010520

ISBN: 1-56309-842-3

N044124 • 1005 • 2M3

Table of Contents

Introduction

by Linda Clark

*I*t was an interesting group I faced that evening. Women had come from all over the state to participate in an annual three-day women's conference. This group was comprised of conference leaders and elected officers of the organization. I knew some of the women, but not much about any of them. We were just a group at that point in time—not a team. Circumstances had brought us together. What tied us together with an unbreakable cord were Christ and a passion for women and their involvement in Kingdom work.

Even with this cord, we were still just a group, perhaps not unlike the band of disciples Jesus gathered around Him during His ministry on earth. Our common desire to share the Good News would keep us together during weeks of transition, several years of re-structuring, and sad times of shared loss among our group. We did not want to remain just a group, however. We wanted to become a team, a team that could be effective in ministering to women in our state. It soon became clear that a team would develop only as its individual members developed as leaders. That realization began an intentional journey to develop equipped leaders who were confident in their abilities and effective in their individual assigned areas of work.

As I look back on those early days, I see God's hand on that group that became a team. These women have felt God's call on their lives to excel in many areas of leadership. Some became national leaders with specialties in age level work. Some became curriculum writers for national mission publications. Others have been chosen to serve on national advisory boards for Christian women's ministry projects and language work. One is currently serving as a vice president of a national women's organization and one served two years as a national officer of an established group of nurses serving in numerous capacities around the world.

Why have these women been so successful in leadership roles? Not only did they feel God's call to ministry, but they had a keen desire to become efficient as well as effective in their work. All of these women were volunteers, so monetary gain did not enter the picture! What did come into play was their commitment to become good stewards of their time, their commitment to be lifelong learners, and their commitment to communicate clearly with women they are training as future leaders.

As I began to reflect on what I considered to be the essentials of leadership, several things came to mind. Through more than thirty years as a women's leader, I have worked with women in local churches—on community projects, in regional settings, and on a national level. I have come to realize that women everywhere have the same basic needs! We all want to have a positive influence on those around us; we all need the fellowship of other Christian women; and all of us desire to use the abilities and talents God has given us. We might not fully understand how God wants to work through us and we may even be hesitant to seek out that will, but the neat thing is that God has a plan for every woman. If she is open to His guidance, she will discover the blessings of being a leader in ways that are unique to her!

Obviously, no two women are alike. When I speak at women's retreats or lead seminars on time management or balancing life's demands, I look out at the women and see such diversity! I'm not thinking just of size, shape, and style. Not even just language differences. I guess I see the potential—the God-given potential—in each of them. God wants us to use our influence for good, to touch others with His love and to be confident in our abilities. While we are unique, we do, however, need some of the same kinds of skills to become effective leaders.

After we titled this book, I did a word search. I discovered some interesting things about the word *essential*. I started with that one word and was given these synonyms: fundamental, key, basic, primary, elementary, central, axiomatic. I chose *key* and continued the search, which resulted in: lock opener (hmmmmm). Then *basic* yielded these words: necessary, root, rudimentary. What about the word *primary?* These words surfaced: principal, chief, main and highest. I took *highest* a step further and got: maximum. From taking *central* to the next level I found: nuclear, pivotal and crucial. Now, *chief* is an easily understood word, I thought . . . leading, prominent. *Prominent* led to *conspicuous,* which led to *salient* and *notable.* I was surprised at the direction *salient* took: distinct, marked, obvious. *Obvious* is related to clear, visible, and evident.

If you followed all of this, you already know where I'm headed! When we talk about essentials of leadership, all of the words listed above are relevant. Many a woman when approached to assume a leadership role wonders if she is equipped to handle the responsibilities she is being asked to perform. She asks herself whether she has the skills to work with others, get her points across, be effective in leading a group, or achieve the desired results.

It doesn't matter whether you are leading a school project, heading a team for a publicity presentation at your firm, or teaching a women's Bible study group. The same leadership skills apply to any leadership role. The five leadership essentials that will be addressed in this book are communication, time management, conflict resolution, relationship building, and group building. Each chapter will deal with one of the essentials and has been designed with women's needs specifically in mind. I pray that you will find something in each chapter that speaks to you and helps you become a more effective leader.

Is leadership important then for women today? Absolutely! As I travel I meet women engaged in a myriad of leadership roles ranging from CEOs to mothers to community volunteers to seminar presenters. All of them have learned along the way the essentials, the basics, of what it means to be a leader. For us as Christian women we know that a dependence upon God is the first step to becoming a leader He can use. When that willingness and faith is in place, then the sky is the limit! He will bless us with opportunities to use our skills and talents beyond our wildest imaginations.

It is my belief that these five leadership essentials will unlock your ability to make things happen!

In His Service,
Linda M. Clark

Note: If you wish to contact me, please email me at: lclark1213@comcast.net

Chapter One

1

Communication Essentials

By Harriet Harral

"You cannot not communicate."

*T*his axiom of communication provides incentive enough for any leader to spend some time studying communication! If we cannot *not* communicate, then we must be communicating all the time. That can be a frightening thought. What myriad messages am I sending to you? What will remain with you? What will you forget even as you turn the page? The answers to these questions are as varied as the readers. That is why the study of communication is so complex and so rewarding, so frustrating, so much fun, so immediate, and so far-reaching.

This section will not answer *all* your questions. It will not make you an expert communicator. My prayer is that it will give you some new ideas and reinforce some old ones. I hope it will alert you to some pitfalls and some opportunities. My goal is to provide you with a ready resource to point out patterns, assist your planning as a leader, and open windows of understanding between you and those with whom you work for the cause of Christ.

In this section you will become better acquainted with biblical women who give evidence that women have been in roles of leadership for centuries and can guide us as we seek to fulfill our responsibilities today. Each part of this chapter will deal with one of the particular communication skills needed by a leader. Learning a new skill involves seeing it modeled, having it explained, trying it ourselves, practicing the skill, and then evaluating how we are doing.

I hope that this discussion of communication will help you to become a leader with more confidence. As you read, keep in mind that an effective communicator always focuses on the receiver. Our focus should always be to lead in such a way that other Christians, as well as non-believers, will see Christ in us.

Say What?
Communication Models

Let me tell you a story. Abigail, an intelligent woman, was the wife of Nabal, a wealthy man who was surly and mean. David and his men arrived in Nabal's territory during the festive time of sheep shearing and approached Nabal with greetings, asking for food. Afraid his servants would leave if he gave away resources, Nabal scornfully refused them and sent them away. David was furious and swore he would kill every male in the household of Nabal.

One of Abigail's servants ran to warn her of the danger from David and explained that David's people had been very kind to them. Abigail immediately gathered donkey-loads of bread, wine, fruit, and grain. Without telling Nabal, she and her servants traveled to David's camp.

As soon as Abigail saw David, she fell to the ground and apologized for her husband's actions. She then acknowledged David's destiny as king and predicted a great future for him. She argued that in his time of success, David would not want on his conscience the staggering burden of needless bloodshed.

Persuaded by Abigail, David thanked her for saving him from the burden of vengefulness. Abigail went home and told Nabal what she had done. His heart failed, and he soon died. When David heard of this, he sent for Abigail to become his wife (this story is based on the Bible story found in 1 Samuel 25).

Abigail was an excellent communicator. She models for us the most effective approach we can take to understand and be understood. Isn't that what communication is all about? It certainly is what this chapter is about!

Yada, Yada, Yada

What are your reactions to the following statements? Think for just a moment about the communication process.

- Communication influences your relationships.
- How you communicate affects your ability to be a good leader.
- Ethical communication demonstrates respect and concern for all involved.
- True communication requires that we accept others' freedom of choice.
- Our attitudes toward others in communication are more significant than the content of the message.

- Choice-making is a part of the communication process.

We choose whether to speak or not to speak. We choose how to say what we choose to say. We choose whether to laugh at, scorn, cry over, or applaud responses to what we say. Sometimes all the options are desirable, and we want them all. Sometimes all the options seem undesirable, and we want *not* to choose. Even that is a choice!

Let's look at three distinct models of communication. Each illustrates the attitudes people have about communication and how they relate to each other as choice-makers. (Remember . . . you *do* have choices!)

#1: One-Way Communication. The first attitude we often see demonstrated about communication says essentially that communication comes from the communicator. It places the entire responsibility for the success of communication on the person sending the message.

In this model, communication is like getting a shot—someone has an idea, squeezes it out through some channel, and squirts it into the receiver. Communication would certainly be easy if it worked that way! Have you ever said anything like this?

- I'm sure they understood me; I repeated my instructions three times.
- She just never makes any sense; I turn her off whenever she starts talking.
- I've got a great speech! It works anywhere.
- No one ever listens to me; I'm a failure.

This philosophy indicates that if a misunderstanding occurs, it must be because the sender didn't say the message right or made some kind of mistake. When people are terrified of giving a speech, they feel that the success of the situation depends entirely on them.

In this kind of thinking about communication, the audience (the receiver) plays no part in the communication process. Their thoughts, feelings, attitudes, and reactions are irrelevant. When the sender takes all the responsibility for the communication, all of the sender's attention is focused on self; there is no attention being given to the reaction or feedback of the receivers.

Nabal exemplifies a one-way attitude toward communication. He was interested only in his own needs and attitudes; he took no time to weigh how his audience, David and his men, might react. He worried about his servants deserting him if he gave food away, but he never stopped to think that they might be distressed at the danger he put them in by making David angry. **A one-way attitude toward communication is self-centered, short-sighted, and inaccurate.**

Answer This:
How do you feel when you are in a situation in which the other person treats communication as all one-way?

Try This:

Place paper and pencil before you, then close your eyes. Keeping your eyes closed, write your name and address in the upper right-hand corner of the page, then draw a map showing where your home is located. Note on the map any points of reference that would be helpful. Look at what you've drawn.

How accurate was your drawing? Your message would probably have been a lot more effective if you had the active participation of a receiver. That is true of *all* communication.

#2: Two-Way Communication. This second model of communication is more realistic than the first because it recognizes the responses we get from others as important. The model looks something like this:

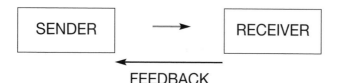

Do you agree with these statements?
- Communication is not just action; it is also reaction.
- Communication is not just stimulus; it is also response.
- A good communicator pays close attention to reactions, or feedback from the receiver.

This is too confusing! I thought I talked, you heard—simple as that! The idea of interaction is an improvement over the action model of communication, but it is still oversimplified. It describes communication as a linear process, one in which a message is sent and then feedback is received. One thing happens, then the next, and so on. This doesn't sound unreasonable until you try to identify stimulus and response, or cause and effect, in a recent conversation you had.

Say you greet someone. What was the stimulus for the greeting? The other person's greeting? Instead of being a response, was your greeting a stimulus to the other person's response? What caused you to say what you did? What caused the other person to say what they said? What did you think the other person's words meant? What did you feel about the way the other person spoke, or the way they looked when speaking?

We could ask all these questions and more about the other person's next comment! Can you distinguish the stimulus and response, the cause and effect? I can't.

Seeing communication as *interaction* is more accurate than seeing it as *action*, but the picture still isn't complete. It doesn't recognize the complete interdependence of the sender and the receiver. I could fulfill the model by speaking awhile and then asking, *Are there any questions?* (adding the feedback loop). But I might still feel that I am responsible to initiate the communication, that I am to be in charge, that I answer your questions in order to make my meaning known to you. Unfortunately, many leaders operate in just this way, not because they are inherently manipulative, but because they have not explored beyond a two-way, interaction model of communication.

David's men demonstrated an interactive approach to communication. They approached Nabal, expecting a particular answer, one favorable to their request, and were unwilling to accept any other. When they received Nabal's negative feedback, they immediately went to David with the bad news. Though all of us would agree that Nabal was surly instead of gracious, he nonetheless had a legitimate concern: servants were leaving their masters, and he was afraid his servants would leave him, too. If David's men had been open to Nabal as a person with a variety of options in the communication situation, they might have been able to negotiate with him. If they had recognized that his response was based on a real concern, they might have helped him avoid what he perceived as negative consequences of their request.

Think About This:

Think of a time when you behaved as if communication were just stimulus/response. What happened? How did you feel? How do you think the other person felt?

Try This:

The next time you are engaged in conversation with a person with whom you feel safe, vary the ways you react to comments they make, and then assess their reactions. For instance, if your friend tells you that she just found a wonderful bargain at a sale, look downcast or out the window as if you are bored. After a brief time, ask her what she thought of your reaction. Discuss the impact you each have on the other when you are in conversation. Ask her what signals she gets from you. Consider the ways in which you influence each other regardless of whether you are the sender or the receiver of the message.

#3: Transactional Communication. This view of communication is the one with the greatest ethical potential. I'll try to explain it by contrasting it with the action and interaction views of communication.

If one views communication as an **action**, the primary concern is with each individual's performance. But communication is more than independent message-sending.

If one views communication as **interaction**, there is a

greater recognition of the full process. Obviously, this view emphasizes feedback, communication as a response to the other person, and how communication continuously involves **mutual and reciprocal influence**. But communication is more than a linear stimulus/response.

Transaction indicates that we construct our views of ourselves, of others, and of meaning as we communicate in relationship with others. A model of transaction would look something like this:

ELEMENTS:
Source
Receiver
Message
Feedback
Environment

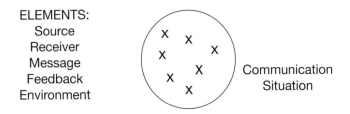

Communication
Situation

Communication is between persons, and it is the *between* that a transactional view tries to recognize. To identify the *between*, a transactional view of communication takes into consideration four important elements.

- **Communication is a process.** Instead of trying to delineate a specific cause or beginning, transaction recognizes that communication is continuous. Our choices are influenced by elements of our past and present that we might not even be aware of. Any communication choice we make does not end once it is completed. It may have ramifications as communication continues. We learn more about ourselves and others and continue to change with them as our communication continues.

- **Communication is a gestalt, a totality depending on all our systems.** Our internal systems (attitudes, emotions, understandings, background, psychological well-being, physical health, etc.) interface with our external systems (situation, time, place, urgency, ritual, etc.) to provide an opportunity to gain understanding. Each new communication situation is unique. Because of what we have learned about ourselves and others in the interim, we view similar situations differently each time we are in them.

- **Communication is perceptual, creative.** No two people perceive the same event in exactly the same way. Our frames of reference are necessarily different because of the differences in our backgrounds, information, interests, attitudes, etc. To the extent that our experiences are similar, we may tend to interpret events similarly. To the extent we differ, our interpretations probably differ.

- **Communication is uncertain.** We can never predict exactly what will happen in a communication situation, can we? Human beings do not provide exact responses to particular stimuli; we are unpredictable.

All four of these elements—**process, totality, perceptions, and uncertainty**—rest on the common assumption that human beings are choice makers. They recognize that we are all free to respond to any given stimulus in any number of ways.

Therefore, the transactional view of communication is an ethical viewpoint, resting on the recognition of freedom of choice. This view indicates the inappropriateness of trying to structure someone else's choices. It points out the necessity of continuing communication with a person in order to learn to share meanings and come to mutually acceptable choices.

How Did Abigail Communicate?

Abigail was a transactional communicator. She understood that this communication took place in an ongoing *process* of communication and could only be assessed in light of the relationship between David, Nabal, and their servants. She looked at the entire situation, its *totality*, and realized the inappropriateness of Nabal's response in light of David's expectations. She immediately tried to understand the message Nabal had sent from the point of view of David's men and knew that the *perception* David and his men would have of Nabal would be extremely negative. She considered Nabal's state of mind and knew that it was not the time to try to reason with him. *Uncertain* as to the outcome, she was willing to risk that in a transaction with David, she could prevail upon his values and attitudes in such a way that he would eventually agree with her.

A Word to Leaders . . .

When leaders behave as though they are responsible for the choices of everyone, there is a significant loss to the group. The danger may be as great as that incurred by Nabal, because such behavior puts the group at risk of dying or stagnating. On the other hand, consider how you feel when your opinions are sought out, when someone listens to you and maybe even changes their mind, when you truly feel that you are connected and involved with another person. That is the goal of the transactional leader.

Answer This:
How do you feel when you are in a situation in which you are treated as a full partner in the communication? Give a recent example of how this occurred.

Hear This . . .

The ethics of communication have to do with our attitudes toward others in any relationship. Those attitudes determine the kind of relationship—and the kind of communication—we will have. To accept the other person and the range of choices, and in so doing to accept our own range of choice—that is the challenge for leaders as they demonstrate ethical communication.

Did You Say What I Heard?

"I know that you believe you understand what you think I said but I am not sure you realize that what you heard is not what I meant."
—Emily Morrison in *Leadership Skills,* p. 89

Why do two different people sometimes have great difficulty in communicating? And why do some people just immediately seem to see the world the same way? Our communication rests on our perceptions of each other and of the world around us. In our earlier discussion about the four elements involved in transactional communication we saw that perception is a personal, individual process drawing on our experiences, attitudes, background, and values. All people see the world from their own vantage point.

Think of the implications these widely differing perceptions have on communication. Sometimes I think it is one of God's great miracles that we can ever understand another person at all!

It can help to have a basic understanding of how the process of perception works. Knowing its structure may help you identify a point at which your perception and that of another person may differ. It may also give you a way to avoid some misunderstandings or to clear up some misperceptions.

When we perceive something, at least four processes are occurring almost simultaneously. Let's look at each of them. Each of the four is followed by an activity you can do to help you further understand how important perception is to the communication process.

Selectivity
We are never able to perceive all of any event.

```
┌─────────────────────────────────────────────────┐
│                    Try This:                     │
│  Sit quietly for a moment. Try to identify everything that │
│  is happening in your environment.               │
│  1. What are the sounds you hear?                │
│  2. What do you see?                             │
│  3. Have you considered everything in all directions? │
│  4. What do you feel? (consider physical sensations │
│  and emotional ones)                             │
│  5. What are the smells around you?              │
│  6. Now consider any other people in your immediate │
│  vicinity. What is each one of them doing, seeing, │
│  hearing, feeling, smelling, etc.?               │
└─────────────────────────────────────────────────┘
```

See how overwhelming it would be to try to perceive all of any event? We select aspects of an event or situation to pay attention to. There will always be other aspects of which we are simply unaware.

Here's another question . . . . How do we select what we perceive? Several factors influence our selection. For instance, there are *physiological factors* that impact our perception. Sometimes we cannot see or hear something clearly. Hearing parts of a conversation, being seated behind a post, or hearing a wreck at the other end of the block are examples where your perception was limited because of physiological factors.

There are also *psychological factors* that influence what we select to perceive. We pay attention to those things that interest us. For instance, if you are driving down the street when you are very hungry, you will probably notice the fast food advertisements. You are interested in anything that says food! We often see what we are interested in seeing. If we want harmony, we will see it. If we are looking for a fight, we will see just those elements that justify the fight.

The third factor influencing how we select what to perceive is *past experience and learning.* Have you ever been in the midst of trying to solve a problem when someone else, maybe unfamiliar with what you were doing, looked at your work, and said, "Why don't you try it this way?" and you suddenly realized they were right? Sometimes we are so familiar with something, so sure we know just how something works, that we are unable to find the creative answer that solves our problem.

Keep in mind that selectivity is not bad. Of course, it can also be the reason for inefficiency, missing important indicators, or completely different understandings of a situation.

Try This:

Choose a situation that is important to you. Ask yourself the following questions to help yourself assess the situation more completely.

1. In what ways might you be physiologically limited in this situation?

2. How are your particular interests influencing your perception?

3. What has been your training and experience regarding this situation? How is that influencing your selections?

4. How would you perceive this situation if you were:
- 12 years old?
- 95 years old?
- from another country?
- unable to speak English?
- the opposite sex?
- a non-Christian?
- a new Christian?
- your mother?
- the person with whom you have difficulty communicating
- Jesus?

Back to the perception process . . . .

Expectation

Once we have selected those aspects of a situation to which we are going to pay attention, the next step in perception is that we begin to make some predictions, or base some expectations on those things we selected. This process is what happens when we stereotype people. Stereotypes are nothing more than predictions about people based on a few, selected characteristics. Expectations are not bad, but we have to be careful not to get locked into a set of expectations. It means that we need to always remember that our perceptions are selective; we never have the whole picture. I saw this slogan on the sign outside a church recently: *Beware of half-truths. You may have the wrong half.* We can use the process of expectation in positive ways as well as negative ones. Expectations can become self-fulfilling prophecies. If we expect the very best of ourselves and others, we often get it!

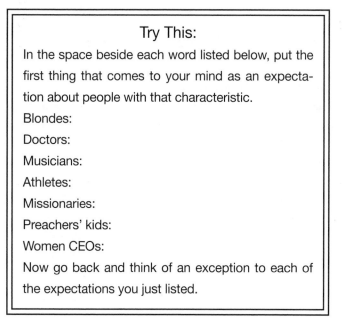

Try This:

In the space beside each word listed below, put the first thing that comes to your mind as an expectation about people with that characteristic.

Blondes:

Doctors:

Musicians:

Athletes:

Missionaries:

Preachers' kids:

Women CEOs:

Now go back and think of an exception to each of the expectations you just listed.

Assess the expectations you have of yourself and others on a regular basis. Be sure that you are not falling into a trap of being too negative or jumping to conclusions based on too few characteristics. Check with other people to find out what they are expecting; then compare notes. Why might they be expecting something very different from you? If your expectations are similar, double-check to see if you have overlooked anything.

Think Again:

1. Identify a leadership situation in which you are trying to be successful.

2. Describe what would be different about yourself if, in fact, you were successful in this situation.

3. Identify someone you know who is feeling uncertain about her leadership abilities at something.

4. List three to five specific ways you can convey to this person that you expect them to be successful.

Emotional Reactions

The third step in perception is an emotional reaction to those selections and expectations. It is not possible to avoid some sort of emotional reaction to any situation we perceive. Some of our reactions are obviously a lot stronger than others. In any case, our emotions influence the totality of our reaction. Sometimes I agree with you because I like you. Sometimes I like you because I agree with you!

When our emotions are particularly strong, we need to be careful that we are not overcome by them. It is hard to continue loving someone when they are doing something that makes us very angry. However, that is what we are commanded to do! We know that Jesus Himself experienced the full range of human emotions. It is all right for us to feel them. Just remember, Jesus did not let Satan manipulate Him even when He was hungry, lonely, and tempted. Our emotions can be a real part of our perceptions without overriding them.

Think About This:

1. List the three things that make you the angriest.
2. How do you usually react when you are really angry?
3. Now, while you are not angry, decide how you would like to react when one of the three things you listed occurs.

Interpretation

We have to make sense for ourselves of what we perceive. The processes of selection, expectation, and emotional reaction happen so quickly that we are usually unaware of them. We become aware at the point that we put it all together into some whole, or gestalt.

Interpretation is not always easy.

• You select characteristics because of your own interests and background.

• You expect certain things because of your selections and because of your experiences with similar situations.

• You react emotionally because of a host of related elements.

No wonder you may understand a situation in a completely different way from someone else! Interpretation is a personal matter but understanding perception will help you identify the spots where you may be differing with someone else. It may help you troubleshoot situations so that you do not end up in misunderstandings that cause problems. It should help you arrive at a fuller, richer understanding by sharing your perceptions with others.

Evaluate Yourself:

Use the following questions to help in any situation, when you want to be sure that you are understanding as fully as possible the situation and the perceptions of the other people involved.

1. List the three things in the situation that seemed the most significant.

2. What do you expect to happen as a result of the situation? Why?

3. What kind of reaction do you expect from the other people involved?

4. How do you feel about the situation? Why?

"I must follow the people.
Am I not their leader?"
—Benjamin Disraeli

"The Line Is Busy.
Call Back Later."
Improving How We Lead

Stop reading and choose which response describes you as a leader right now.

- "You have the wrong number."
- "This number has been disconnected."
- "There's no one here by that name."
- "This party accepts no calls without caller ID."
- "The line is busy. Call back later."

The Old Testament judge Deborah may have wished for an excuse not to lead out at some point, but she was a prophetess and judge in the hill country of Ephraim and the Israelites obviously trusted her, for they came to her to have their disputes settled. For twenty years the Israelites had been oppressed by a cruel military commander, Sisera. Deborah sent Barak specific instructions to lead the way with ten thousand troops to Mount Tabor in order to engage Sisera in battle. Barak agreed to go only if Deborah would go with him. Barak followed Deborah's instructions and defeated Sisera's army. Deborah wrote and sang a song of celebration for the great national victory (based on Judges 4–5).

Deborah is a woman who demonstrates the very best principles of an approach to leadership called situational leadership. Taking into account the needs of the people she was leading, she changed her style in order to help them grow in the tasks she assigned them. Situational leadership, a model developed by Ken Blanchard and Paul Hersey, can give us guidance regarding the communication style to use in a given situation.

Leaders can be leaders, after all, only if their followers follow them! That means leaders must be carefully tuned in to the needs of their followers (no disconnected numbers!). If a leader meets a person's needs, that person will be extremely loyal. Too often leaders begin to think that followers are supposed to meet the leader's needs (no busy lines!).

Look over you shoulder . . . . is anyone following?

There is no one perfect leadership or communication approach. What is effective depends on the situation, the needs of the people involved, and the job the leader is asking them to do. The leader must assess the specific task in a given situation and determine the **ability** and the **willingness** of the individual or group being asked to accomplish it.

Ability. Is the individual capable of doing the task? Has she ever done it before? Has she been trained? If so, little information or direction is needed from the leader. If not, the worker needs more communication, attention, and assistance from the leader.

Willingness. Is the worker confident of her ability to do the task? Is she comfortable with the assignment? Does she want to do it? If the answers to these questions are yes, the worker needs less encouragement and support from the leader than if any of the answers are no.

As you as a leader determine the ability and willingness of a member of your team, you will become more effective, and in turn, your team will move toward accomplishing its purpose.

```
┌─────────────────────────────────────────────┐
│              Think About This:                │
│ 1. Think of a time when you were asked to take on a │
│ responsibility you had never done before. What was │
│ your first reaction?                           │
│ 2. What kind of support did you get from your  │
│ leader?                                        │
│ 3. Think of a time when you were asked to do a task │
│ you had done many times before. What was your  │
│ reaction?                                      │
│ 4. What kind of questions did you have? What did │
│ you need from your leader in that situation? What │
│ support did you get?                           │
│                                                │
└─────────────────────────────────────────────┘
```

There are many books on the market today that discuss the various approaches to leadership, all of which involve specific communication approaches as well. Let's look at four that can be related to the biblical story of the Old Testament judge Deborah.

Telling

If the individual or group has a low level of ability and/or willingness, the leader will need to give a lot of emphasis to the task—specific instructions about what needs to be done, when it should be done, how it should be done, and who should do it. This could involve: staying in close touch; setting up frequent reports or meetings; providing manuals with detailed information; pairing a new leader with an experienced one as a model; and setting deadlines.

Deborah functioned in a *telling* fashion when she gave Barak specific instructions. Barak evidently was either unwilling or felt unable to accomplish the task alone. In fact, he said he would follow Deborah's instructions only if she went with him. Deborah recognized he would not be able to succeed alone and agreed to go with him (Judges 4:8–10).

Coaching

When an individual or group begins to develop a bit more experience and willingness, the leader can move to a style that is a little less directive and a little more supportive. A coach gives direction but also provides encouragement and support. Encourage those you have asked to take on responsibilities, give them feedback, and use debriefing sessions that include celebration of successes.

Barak became more confident as he and Deborah were followed by ten thousand men. Deborah moved to a coaching style when she urged him, "Go! This is the day the LORD has given Sisera into your hands. Has not the LORD gone ahead of you?" (Judges 4:14).

Encouraging

A group or an individual with a good bit of experience and willingness to do a task is usually eager to have a say in how the task is done. Not needing much instruction or supervision, the leader can facilitate their moving into a leadership role of their own.

During the time of Jabin, the evil king of Canaan, Deborah was Israel's leader. My guess is that she used encouragement as a primary style of communication with her people. The people came to her for help in deciding their disputes, and this sounds like she empowered them to be involved in those decisions. After the defeat of Sisera, she joined Barak in a song of great jubilation. She recognized her role in the triumph, but she also paid homage to others who were involved (Judges 5).

Delegating

Truly experienced, capable, and eager individuals or groups are able to take on the responsibility of the task, leaving the leader to spend time on other tasks or with other groups who are at lower levels of ability and willingness. Allow your leaders to be in charge unless they come to you with requests for assistance.

Deborah knew from the first that Sisera would be defeated by a woman (Judges 4:9) and was obviously willing to leave that entirely up to Jael. Jael was the wife of Heber the Kenite, from a clan that had peaceful relations with Jabin the king. Sisera clearly went to her because he thought she would provide a safe hiding spot. She didn't hesitate in carrying out her plan to destroy Sisera. Capable of the task, she carried it out without direction or encouragement!

Try This:

Think of one of your groups—Bible study, missions, team at work—which calls for one of these leadership approaches. Describe a situation, explaining why the particular approach is appropriate in light of the willingness and ability of the followers in that specific instance. Explain specific actions you as the leader should take in that situation.

1. Telling:

2. Coaching:

3. Encouraging:

4. Delegating:

Is your line still busy? Do your followers need caller ID? Or have you discontinued service?

The following questions may help you evaluate a project your group is working on right now. Evaluation is critical in order to clarify unaddressed issues, unspoken needs, and inadequate communication. Don't just fill in the blanks! Think about your answers.

1. Were the specific goals of this task clear? Yes ___ No ___
2. What specifically made the goal so clear or unclear?
3. Did you have an understanding of what you were supposed to do on this task?
4. What did the leader do that helped you?
5. Did you receive encouragement and support in accomplishing this task? Yes ___ No ___
6. In what specific ways were you encouraged and supported?
7. Next time, what would you suggest to help the leader improve? (Answer this even if you were the leader!)

Remember . . .

- No leader is perfect, but the most effective leaders remember that people perform best when their needs are met.
- A good leader asks questions and listens carefully to insure that she can offer the direction and the support most needed by her team.
- She helps her followers do their very best by choosing the appropriate leadership approach in any given situation.

Can You Hear Me Now? Listening

The mother went to the back door one more time and called her daughter. No response. She knew she'd been heard. The daughter knew she'd been called. No response. With other more pressing things to do, the mother went about her work and finally, in her own time, the little girl came inside. "Mama, I'd have come if I'd heard you calling!" Hmmmm. Sounds as if "someone" wasn't listening. She'd heard her mother's voice but didn't really listen.

Listening may be the most important part of communication. It may not have occurred to you that more time is spent in listening than in talking, reading, or writing. Most of us spent a great deal of time learning to read and write. Some of us took speech classes or received some oral assignments. Very few of us have had any formal training in listening. It is through listening that we validate each other. It is through listening that we create the opportunity to truly know each other.

An excellent example of listening is Mary, the sister of Martha and Lazarus of Bethany. It was to their house that Jesus went for fellowship and rest. Martha, the elder of the sisters, took her responsibilities as hostess very seriously. Jesus brought His disciples with Him, so there were a number of people to feed and prepare for. She worked hard getting ready for them, and serving them after they arrived.

Mary was also excited about Jesus' visit. Her focus, however, was on the opportunity to be with Jesus Himself. She was so eager to be with Him that, even though women usually did not sit with men, she joined the group with Him in order to just listen to what He had to say. After a time, Martha became frustrated with the responsibilities she had assumed and was shouldering alone. She went to Jesus, asking Him to tell Mary to help her. Jesus responded that Mary had chosen the better thing to do, to listen and learn of Him (based on Luke 10: 38–42).

Listener Profiles

We all know people who are good listeners, and we certainly won't forget the poor listeners we've come across. Here are the profiles of both types:

Good Listeners: friendly, open, warm, empathetic, patient, honest, sincere.

Bad Listeners: closed, impatient, nervous, angry, unwilling to change.

Good listening is critical to becoming a good leader. A leader must be aware of the skill level and willingness of people to do various tasks. Through good listening, a leader can have the information necessary to make wise decisions about how best to lead in a given situation.

The following exercises are opportunities to assess your own listening skills, identify some typical listening problems, and work toward increasing listening effectiveness.

"Many attempts to communicate are nullified by saying too much."
—Robert Greenleaf, in *Servant Leadership*

- List the three best listeners you know and the characteristics of each.
- Do you dislike any of them?
- List three of the worst listeners you know and the characteristics of each.

Now . . . How Well Do You Listen?
Take a few minutes to think about your listening skills. Think about a conversation you've had recently. Then answer as honestly as you can.
1. What were you thinking about as the other person was speaking?
2. Were you really hearing what the person was saying, or were you adding your own interpretation?
3. How do your attitudes about the speaker or the topic of conversation affect your listening skills?
4. How do hidden messages or unspoken communication affect the way you respond in a conversation?

Obstacles to Effective Listening

When Wayne was in elementary school he had a high aversion to vegetables, especially green beans. From his point of view, the only good green bean was one on its way to the garbage disposal! When we would try to convince him to eat them at dinnertime, he would hold his fingers in his ears and repeat over and over in a loud voice, "I can't hear you! I can't hear you! I can't hear you!" Certainly an obstacle to listening!

Let's look at a series of specific behaviors and/or attitudes that act as barriers to effective listening.

1. Focus on self. Often during interactions with others, we are more concerned about what we are saying or going to say than what the other person is saying. Our thoughts fly ahead to plan our reaction to what is being said to the extent that sometimes we actually miss the comment to which we think we are responding! What's the antidote?

• Clear your mind and practice concentrating on the other person.

• Make an effort to send the impression that you are paying complete attention.

2. Wandering mind. The average speaker talks at a rate of about 200 words per minute. We are capable of thinking at a rate of about 400 words per minute. Consequently, our minds might do a myriad of things other than concentrate on what the other person is saying. What's the antidote?

• Develop examples of the speaker's ideas.
• Develop questions.
• Mentally summarize what you have heard.
• Apply what you are hearing to specific situations.

3. Leveling. As we listen, there is often a tendency to simplify the message we are hearing in order to remember it better. That is the process of leveling. The problem is that we may omit details which are critical or which seem unimportant to us, thereby distorting the intent of the message. What's the antidote?

• Listen carefully to avoid leveling, perhaps taking notes.
• Compare what you heard with another person.
• Ask questions of the speaker, to be sure that you have the message correct.

4. Sharpening. Certain things in any message stand out over other things. When we pass the message on to someone else, the likelihood is that we will emphasize those particular points. We may even embellish them, and in the process, leave out other important information. That is the process of sharpening. What's the antidote?

• The strategies listed for leveling also can be useful for

avoiding sharpening.

5. Assimilation. In this process, we tend to shape messages so that they confirm our own opinions or attitudes. The political "spin doctors" are examples of this. Sometimes we tend to assume that the other person's attitudes are the same as our own; therefore they must mean what we would mean if we were speaking. What's the antidote?
- Practice active listening.
- Listen from the other person's point of view.
- Ask yourself, *What could this message mean?*

6. Hearing what is expected. Sometimes we are sure that we know what another person thinks or feels about an issue. We are so sure that we neglect to listen when they talk about it. What's the antidote?
- Be careful that you don't just hear what you expect to hear.
- Work at keeping an open mind.

7. Passive listening. Passive listening is the tendency to view the interaction as an event to which you are simply an audience. A passive listener tunes in and out, picking and choosing only parts of the message. Such a listener rarely develops a clear understanding of other people and their needs. What's the antidote?
- Active listening—paraphrase what the speaker is saying, respond to the feelings of the speaker, and ask questions.

8. Missing the meaning. We typically miss the meaning a speaker intended when we concentrate on the content of the message but neglect to think about the feelings behind it. Or we evaluate or judge the speaker or the message before working for full understanding. The third barrier is to be too literal and thus miss more subtle meanings. What's the antidote?
- Listen for clues about the speaker's intentions and feelings.
- Think about relationship messages as well as content messages.

- Be sure to defer judgment until you have heard the entire message and double-checked to be sure you understand its intention.

Think About This

For each of the following situations, write out how you would paraphrase, respond to feelings, and ask questions.

Situation: "I can't possibly take this position next year. I had that job once and it was a disaster. Nobody was ever willing to help, and I got stuck with doing almost all of the programs by myself."

Paraphrase:

Respond to Feelings:

Ask Questions: Would it make a difference this time if you had a co-chairperson?

Situation: "I know I've missed a lot of meetings lately, but I've been busy, and besides, nobody called or anything so I didn't think anyone missed me."

Paraphrase:

Respond to Feelings:

Ask Questions:

Lend Me Your Ear!
Ten Tips for Effective Listening

Brenda Ueland suggests ten steps we can take to improve our listening skills.

1. Stop talking! As long as you are talking, you cannot be listening.

2. Behave as you think a good listener should behave:

- Put the speaker at ease.
- Show you are interested.
- Establish good eye contact.
- Give nonverbal signals that you are paying attention.
- Be patient. Give the speaker plenty of time.
- Don't react emotionally.

3. Listen for the main points. Build a mental outline. Take notes if that helps.

4. Concentrate. Keep your total focus on the person speaking.

5. Be open-minded. Don't make up your mind in advance about what the speaker will say or how you will react to it even if you disagree. Then assess the conflicting ideas carefully to determine where you want to stand on the issue.

6. Watch out for words that elicit emotional reactions from you. We all have signal reactions to certain words. Identify those words for yourself and slow down your reactions to them. Force yourself to get past the words in order to understand the person speaking them.

7. Defer judgment. Wait until you have heard and are sure you understand the entire message before you make decisions.

8. Listen empathetically. Seek to approach the message from the other person's perspective instead of your own.

9. Ask questions. Questions show your interest and encourage the speaker as well as clarifying the message for you.

10. Stop talking!

Back to Mary . . . .

Mary was a listener who instinctively knew the techniques of good listening. She was quiet, responsive, and supportive of Jesus as He spoke and taught. We know that her entire focus was on Jesus, even to the point of forgetting the norms of the times and her responsibilities as a hostess. We know that she listened well and absorbed His meaning, because Jesus commended her.

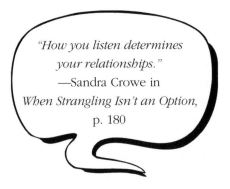

"How you listen determines your relationships."
—Sandra Crowe in
When Strangling Isn't an Option,
p. 180

I See What You're Saying! Unspoken Communication

Dorcas was part of an active Christian community in Joppa, and evidently provided a great deal of leadership in reaching out to minister to the poor. She was known as someone who was always doing good. Dorcas became ill and died. Those who loved her prepared her body for burial and placed her in an upstairs room. Hearing that the apostle Peter was in Lydda, not too far away, they sent for him, asking him to come at once. Whether they wanted him there because they thought he could perform a miracle, or because he should be there for the burial, we don't know. We do know that Peter went right away.

When Peter arrived at the upstairs room, it was filled with widows, who showed him the robes and other clothing Dorcas had made. After sending everyone out of the room, Peter knelt and prayed. Then he turned to Dorcas and asked her to rise. She opened her eyes and sat up. Peter called everyone back in and presented Dorcas to them. This event became known all over Joppa, and many people believed in the Lord (based on Acts 9:36–42).

Dorcas sent significant messages through her behavior to people who knew her. She gave to others, she did for others, and she cared about people in need. Her life served as a witness to her faith and spoke more loudly to those around her than anything she might have said. Dorcas witnessed nonverbally as she gave of herself to others. Without words, she preached the message of Jesus.

What You're Doing Speaks So Loudly That I Can't Hear What You Are Saying

Researchers in the field of communication claim that nonverbal communication, such as facial expressions and the ways words are said, relay more information than do spoken words. Joyce Mitchell in her book *Teams Work!* estimates that only 7 percent of meaning in a conversation is verbal. That means that 93 percent is nonverbal! Of that 93 percent, tone and inflection (the way words are said) account for 38 percent, with 55 percent being facial expression.

Nonverbal communication covers a host of forms of communication. In fact, it involves so many things that it has been said that we cannot *not* communicate. Think about that for a minute. Even a refusal to communicate communicates something!

Our nonverbal communication often is unintentional. Have you ever had someone come up to you and ask, "What's wrong?" You weren't intending to convey distress, but something about your expression sent that signal. Our clothes, the condition of our desk and office, our housekeeping style, the appearance of our yard, the time we spend in certain activities—these are all ways we communicate whether we intend to or not. Our Christian witness is often the product of unintentional messages. These can be the strongest messages we send!

In this section, we will be looking at the functions of nonverbal communication and at a variety of forms of body language.

Try This:

Watch a conversation from a distance. Based on facial expression, body language, and tone of voice (if you can hear the sounds of the voices), make up what you think the content of the conversation is. What are the attitudes of the people involved?

How Does Nonverbal Communication Work?

Nonverbal communication can function in at least three different ways.

First, it augments verbal communication. We use gestures and tone of voice to emphasize ideas, to show emotion, to make something funnier. Gestures might be waving one's hands, pointing, or drawing in the air. Tone of voice can show emotions or humor.

Second, we may use nonverbal communication instead of verbal communication. Sometimes we are unable to talk (for example, when someone else is speaking, when we don't know the language, or when we don't want to be heard). We nonetheless convey messages in a number of ways. There are formalized ways of using nonverbal communication to replace verbal such as sign language with the deaf.

A **third** form of nonverbal communication contradicts the verbal message. When there is a contradiction between verbal and nonverbal messages, which do you think is more important? That may be a hard question to answer in the abstract. Consider this: your best friend comes running up to you with a huge smile, gives you a great bearhug, and says, "I could just kill you!" Do you feel threatened? Probably not. You would probably assume that your friend is being very affirming, perhaps about to chastise you for some particularly nice thing you have done.

If a verbal message and a nonverbal message contradict each other, we almost always will believe the nonverbal message.

Back to our biblical model . . .

Consider Dorcas and the nonverbal messages she sent as she sewed for those in need. Did her messages augment her verbal witness? Did they substitute for spoken messages? Or did they contradict her other messages? We don't know a lot about Dorcas' verbal interactions with others. We do know that her behavior spoke for itself. Her behavior complemented her

Christian commitment, and it may well have stood on its own as a substitute for more assertive forms of witness. In no way did Dorcas' behavior contradict the Christian principles by which she lived.

Try This:

Experiment with these ideas.

1. In your mirror at home, practice a variety of ways to contradict a verbal message you are planning to deliver. Then try delivering it nonverbally. Based on those experiences, determine the best ways to use nonverbal communication to augment your message.

2. Assess the nonverbal messages at one of your group or team meetings. What messages are being sent without words?

Excuse Me,
Did You Just Point at Me?

Because nonverbal communication is so much a part of all our interactions with others, let's look briefly at the varieties of forms in which it occurs.

Body Language. Body language is probably the first thing that comes to mind when we think of nonverbal communication. It carries significant levels of meaning. Five specific types of body language can be identified to help us make choices about the messages we send and the meanings of the messages we receive.

1. Emblems are nonverbal behaviors that stand for an idea—a wave, a hitchhiker's thumb, or praying hands.

2. Illustrators go along with the spoken word and help a receiver understand it by providing a visual demonstration of it—measuring with our hands, pointing to something, or pacing out a distance.

3. Affect displays are facial expressions that show an emotional reaction or state—a grimace, smile, frown, raised eyebrows. These facial expressions may be unintentional, and give away clues to our inner feelings. Sometimes we intentionally use facial expressions to convey our feelings!

4. Regulators are used in conversations to monitor or regulate the flow of the discussion—nodding our head, making eye contact, leaning forward. These either encourage a speaker to continue or signal them to stop.

5. Adaptors are behaviors that usually indicate an inner state and are an unconscious response—like rubbing your neck when under stress.

Space Communication. The way we place ourselves in relationship to others conveys a great deal about our feelings toward the other person, and about our cultural norms. The more formal our relationships, the more distance we put between ourselves.

This use of space is definitely tied to one's culture. In some countries, people relate at completely different distances from each other. Touching in one culture is not done while in another there is a great deal more touching.

Time Communication. Time is another dimension that is bound to culture. There are at least three ways we use time to communicate:

1. Formal time—those aspects of time that we establish in our culture as meaningful, such as seconds, minutes, and hours. In other cultures, the significant units may be phases of the moon or seasons.

2. Informal time—references to pieces of time when we say *awhile, in just a second, a long time,* and *as soon as possible.* These units of time provide opportunity for misunderstanding even within our own culture because they are inexact. Learning the informal units of time in another culture is even more difficult.

3. Psychological time—the significance we place on the past, present, and future. This may vary from individual to individual, or from group to group within a culture. It certainly varies from culture to culture.

Artifactual Communication. Some nonverbal communication comes from the objects we use or with which we surround ourselves: the way we dress or accessorize ourselves, the type of house we choose, the cars we drive, and so forth. A great deal of emphasis has been given in recent years to dress, especially for women in professional contexts. All artifacts we choose say something about us.

Think About Your Nonverbal Communication

Ask someone to evaluate your nonverbal communication the next time you make a presentation, lead a seminar or direct a meeting.

1. What did my voice convey about the message and my feelings about it?
2. How should I try to improve my voice?
3. What did my body language convey about me and/or the message?
4. How could I improve my body language?
5. What did my clothing, accessories, etc. convey about my message and/or about me?
6. How can I improve my dress, accessories, etc. to convey a more positive message?

Remember . . . . Our behavior also communicates. Learning to send nonverbal messages that speak truly of our inner efforts to live our faith is a worthy attempt. Remember to witness nonverbally as well as verbally.

Public Speaking or Death? Death, Please!

A survey a few years ago revealed that for many people, the fear of speaking before a group was greater than fears of height, financial problems, deep water, sickness, and dying. When some people say, *I'd rather die than give a speech*, they are telling the literal truth!

Nonetheless, the ability to speak articulately and persuasively before a group is one of the more important skills a leader needs. In this section, we will work on the following basic skills for increasing your confidence as a public speaker: dealing with speech apprehension, using nonverbal strategies, and focusing on the audience.

Does the Bible Have a Role Model for Women Leaders? Absolutely!

Priscilla and her husband Aquila were Christian tentmakers with a burning missionary drive. They welcomed Paul to stay in their home when he left Athens and went to Corinth. Paul, also a tentmaker, felt comfortable with them. He stayed in Corinth for a year and a half, preaching and working with his friends. When he left to go to Ephesus, Priscilla and Aquila sailed with him.

After a time, Paul left them in charge of the church in Ephesus. Their home became the meeting place for the group of Christians. Priscilla and Aquila took a young scholar, Apollos, under their wings, teaching him more fully the truths of Christianity.

Paul's letters to the churches at Rome and Corinth, as well as his letter to Timothy, mention Priscilla and Aquila with great fondness, and he credits them with saving his life (based on Acts 18; Romans 16:3; 1 Corinthians 16:19; 2 Timothy 4:19).

These brief pieces of information about Priscilla imply a great deal. In a society in which women were second-class citizens, she is consistently mentioned before her husband. Her name is found on monuments in Rome. Tertullian, an early church father, mentioned her as "the holy Prisca, who preached the gospel." Tradition credits her with a book, the *Acts of St. Prisca*, and some even credit her with the authorship of the Epistle to the Hebrews. She was, without doubt, a woman able to effectively and persuasively develop a message.

Can You Hear My Knees Knocking?

What abilities did Priscilla possess that we as female leaders might develop to become more effective in our public speaking? Before any of us can become a persuasive speaker, we must look at the apprehension we feel when called upon to make a presentation, lead a workshop, or speak before a group of women.

The usual term for nervousness before an audience is *stage fright*. That term, however, implies that fear is present. Now think a minute about how you feel when you are nervous about speaking. Are you actually *afraid* of the audience or the situation? Do you really *fear* that they are going to do something harmful to you? Probably not. What you are feeling is the very normal reaction of a conscientious person who wants to do a good job.

Because of that, speech teachers have begun using the terms *speech apprehension* or *speech anxiety* to refer to those feelings before giving a speech. Fear occurs when there is a real, external stimulus. Anxiety usually relates to internal qualities rather than external events. A person is afraid of a criminal; they have anxiety about their ability to fit in at a new job. All of this is to say that you are really not scared about public speaking; you want to do your best. And that is good!

The tips to follow about dealing with anxiety will not eliminate it; they will help you deal with it. Take your responsibility to an audience seriously and do your best. Enjoy the added energy and enthusiasm that comes from your apprehension of the situation.

Assess Your Apprehension

For each statement, indicate the response that seems most appropriate for you. These responses should be your first impressions. Indicate your responses on a scale of one to five (1=strongly agree; 2=agree; 3=undecided; 4=disagree; 5=strongly disagree).[1]

_____ 1. While participating in a conversation with a new acquaintance, I feel very nervous.

_____ 2. I have no fear of facing an audience.

_____ 3. I talk less because I'm shy.

_____ 4. I look forward to expressing my opinions at meetings.

_____ 5. I am afraid to express myself in a group.

_____ 6. I look forward to an opportunity to speak in public.

_____ 7. I find the prospect of speaking mildly pleasant.

_____ 8. When communicating, my posture feels strained and unnatural.

_____ 9. I am tense and nervous while participating in group discussion.

_____ 10. Although I talk fluently with friends, I am at a loss for words on the platform.

_____ 11. I have no fear about expressing myself in a group.

_____ 12. My hands tremble when I try to handle objects on the platform.

_____ 13. I always avoid speaking in public if possible.

_____ 14. I feel that I am more fluent when talking to others than most people are.

_____ 15. I am fearful and tense the entire time I am speaking before a group of people.

_____ 16. My thoughts become confused and jumbled when I speak to groups.

_____ 17. I like to get involved in group discussions.

_____ 18. Although I am nervous just before getting up, I soon forget my fears and enjoy the experience.

_____ 19. Conversing with people who hold positions of authority causes me to be fearful and tense.

_____ 20. I dislike using my body and voice expressively.

_____ 21. I feel relaxed and comfortable when speaking.

_____ 22. I feel self-conscious when I am called upon to answer a question or give an opinion in a group.

_____23. I face the prospect of making a speech with complete confidence.

_____24. I'm afraid to speak up in conversation.

_____25. I would enjoy presenting a speech on a local television show.

To Score: Compute your score in the following way:
1. Add up your scores for items 1, 3, 5, 8, 9, 10, 12, 13, 15, 16, 19, 20, 22, and 24: _____

2. Add up your scores for items 2, 4, 6, 7, 11, 14, 17, 18, 21, 23, and 25: _____

3. Complete the following formula to find your Apprehension Score: 84—_____ (total from Step 1) + _____ (total from Step 2)

Interpreting Your Score: Scores of 88 or higher would indicate considerable apprehension. Scores between 75 and 87 would indicate some apprehension. Scores below 74 would indicate little apprehension.

1From McCrosky, James C. and Wheeless, Lawrence R., *Introduction to Human Communication.* Copyright © 1976 by Allyn and Bacon. Adapted by permission.

My Knees Are Still Knocking!

Another way to think about speech apprehension is to understand it as a normal reaction to a potentially threatening situation. Our bodies are prepared to deal with a threat by either running away or fighting. You have probably heard about *fight or flight.*

In other words, when we feel speech apprehension, we can be assured that our bodies are preparing in the most efficient way possible for us to be at our best. Our muscles tense for agility, our heartbeat and breathing increase to provide more fuel, our glands secrete fluids to sharpen our senses and give us energy. This process is a great gift from God!

Unfortunately, when this happens, we think, *Oh, no! I'm scared!* What we should be thinking is, *Wonderful! My body is operating at top condition. I am ready for anything!*

The only difficulty is that when we are in a public speaking situation, we really are not supposed to fight or to flee. We have to stay right there, looking completely under control with our bodies revved up like crazy! We experience symptoms of nervousness because our bodies are ready to do something extremely active, yet we are standing still.

Consider these nervous symptoms. Think about your own nervous symptoms and which ones are present when you are in a public speaking situation.

- Voice (quivering, too fast, too slow, monotone)
- Verbal fluency (stammering, halting, vocalized pauses, speech blocks)
- Mouth and throat (swallowing, clearing throat, heavy breathing, dryness)
- Facial expression (lack of eye contact, eyes everywhere, tense face muscles, twitches, blushing)
- Arms and hands (rigid, tense, fidgeting, shaking hands, hands in pockets or hair, sweaty palms)
- Legs and feet (swaying, shuffling feet, pacing, knocking knees)

If you look back at your various symptoms, you can see that almost all of them are examples of your body trying to work off the excess energy it has generated. Your muscles have tensed in preparation for action. If you have a sinking feeling in your stomach, it is because your body is generating adrenalin and other glandular secretions. When that happens, the process of digestion stops and your stomach contracts, causing the sinking sensation.

It is not practical to talk of eliminating the symptoms of speech apprehension! Your goal should be to control those symptoms.

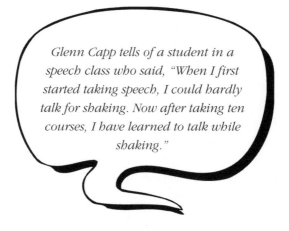

Glenn Capp tells of a student in a speech class who said, "When I first started taking speech, I could hardly talk for shaking. Now after taking ten courses, I have learned to talk while shaking."

Help Me Control The Shaking!

1. *Know your own reactions.* Look back at the list of nervous symptoms.

2. *Develop a plan for dealing with each symptom.* If your palms sweat, keep a handkerchief in your pocket. If your mouth gets dry, have a glass of water handy.

3. *If you have trouble with shaking hands or legs just before speaking, work off the excess energy.* If possible, do some physical exercise before you give a speech. Swing your arms, jog in place, do knee bends, rotate your neck and head. If you are unable to hide to do exercises, try isometric exercises just before speaking. Tense your muscles as hard as you can, and then release them.

4. *Care about your audience.* Instead of thinking about yourself and how you are doing, consciously think about the audience. Watch them to see if they are interested and strive to interest them in what you are saying.

5. *Develop some good memory aids.* Do not write out your speech word for word because you will be tempted to read it word for word. Speak from an outline, using notes with notations of important points.

6. *Do some preliminary work to reduce any worries you may have.* Arrive early. Dress in something that is comfortable and makes you feel good. Meet some people ahead of time so that you see friendly faces as you speak.

7. *Practice, practice, practice.* Nothing helps your confidence more than knowing what you are going to do and say. Practice aloud and in front of a mirror.

8. *Seek out opportunities to give speeches.* (Yes, you read that right!) Your skill and confidence will grow with experience.

9. *Remember, you are engaged in God's work.* He is there to support you.

Look me in the eye. The most important thing you can do as a speaker is establish good eye contact with your audience. This allows you to show that you care about them. Eye contact also conveys the message that you are a credible speaker.

Tips about making eye contact: Establish eye contact with a single individual and maintain it for five seconds before you move your eyes to look at someone else. As you change eye contact, move across the room in a zigzag, or Z shape, so that all parts of the room are covered. Spend five seconds in contact with each person.

My voice is all wrong. The next important part of your speech is the sound of your voice. *How* you say what you say carries more meaning than the words themselves. Speakers who are dynamic and who have vocal variety are thought to be more credible than speakers who speak in monotone. The increased rate of speaking and the increased pitch variety convey a sense of animation and dynamism.

Tips about voice skills:

• If you are really committed, enthusiastic, and care about your audience, it will show in your voice. You cannot care passionately about something and speak in a monotone.

• Add stories, examples, and instances to your presentation. You'll become more energetic vocally when you tell a story.

• Listen to yourself on a tape recorder. Keep in mind there are three primary vocal characteristics you can control:

1. Pitch—A high pitch conveys uncertainty, immaturity, and a lack of substance. If your voice is high-pitched, you can lower it a tone or two by consciously practicing and listening to yourself.

Try This:

1. Count to five in your normal speaking voice.

2. Begin again at that same pitch, but lower your voice a tone on each number as you count to five.

3. Count to five again, beginning at your normal tone, and raise your voice a pitch with each number.

4. Read the following passage from the song sung by Miriam, Moses, and Aaron. Follow the changes in pitch as indicated.

(*Normal*) I will sing to the LORD, for he is highly exalted.

(*Lower*) The horse and its rider he has hurled into the sea.

(*Normal*) The LORD is my strength and my song; he has become my salvation.

(*Higher*) He is my God and I will praise him,

(*Normal*) my father's God, and I will exalt him. (Exodus 15:1–2)

---

2. Pace—We can learn to control the pace of our speaking. No one likes to listen to a constant, unchanging speaking voice. A fairly rapid rate of speech sends the message that you are more animated, that you are more interested in your audience, and that you are more credible. It is better to speak a little too fast than too slowly, but remember that it is very easy in public speaking to talk too fast; what sounds normal to you can sound fast to your audience. Strive for variety in your pacing. Change pace to signal to your audience that something significant is about to be said.

Try This Too!

1. Watch the clock and speak as quickly as you can to see how far you can count in five seconds.

2. Now see how slowly you can count and still sound normal. At that rate, how far would you count in five seconds?

3. Read the following passage about the deliverance at the Red Sea, changing rate as indicated. How does the rate change impact the meaning?

(*Very slow*) Your right hand, O LORD, was majestic in power.

(*Slow*) Your right hand, O LORD, shattered the enemy.

(*Normal*) In the greatness of your majesty you threw down those who opposed you.

(*Faster*) You unleashed your burning anger; it consumed them like stubble.

(*Faster*) By the blast of your nostrils the waters piled up.

(*Slower*) The surging waters stood firm like a wall;

(*Slower*) the deep waters (*even slower*) congealed (*a little faster*) in the heart of the sea. (Exodus 15:6–8)

---

3. Inflection—Force, tone, and pitch variations are all part of inflection. Effective speakers use these elements to capture interest.

Say the following sentence aloud: *I would not say we lost the fight.*
Now, varying the inflection, continue to say the sentence aloud:

I would not say we lost the fight.
I would not *say* we lost the fight.
I would not say *we* lost the fight.
I would not say we *lost* the fight.
I would not say we lost the *fight.*

The words remained the same in each sentence, but the meaning changed as you changed the inflection, or emphasis, you placed on the words.

Again . . .
1. Speak the sentence, "He did that," and suggest the following different meanings: ask a question; demonstrate shock, delight, and sarcasm.
2. Say "Hello" in a variety of ways to express warmth, surprise, disgust, shame.

Speakers, Audiences, & Messages— Which Comes First?

As a speaker, you have three choices of focus in a public speaking situation: your message, yourself, or your audience.

1. Message-centered communication—makes the content the most important. Don't waste an audience's time with less than the best you have in the way of ideas and information.

2. Speaker-centered communication—focuses on the

speaker and what she is saying. Speakers should know their content and be comfortable in their delivery.

3. Audience-centered communication—focuses on the audience and how it receives the message. It is the most important of the three approaches. A speaker who really cares about her listeners and shows it is way ahead in terms of focus.

Hints for Analyzing Your Audience

• **Find out what your audience knows about your topic.** The more you know about your audience's knowledge of the topic, the better able you are to determine your level of speaking. Don't embarrass yourself by talking only about those things that an audience already knows, or which are so difficult that the audience cannot understand them.

• **Determine your audience's attitude about your topic.** Are they excited about it? Did they come because of the topic? Don't let yourself get blindsided by attitudes you didn't know were there!

• **Ask yourself what the audience knows about you.** Do you share something in common with them? It is always appropriate to be introduced, so provide information for the introducer.

• **Find out as much as you can about the people making up the audience.** Ask the person who has invited you to speak to give you information about them. Knowing the audience's age span; gender; race; or family, economic, religious, or political status will help you prepare your comments.

Think About a Specific Situation

Think about an upcoming presentation you are making or a seminar you are leading. Do you know the answers to the following questions?

1. Is there anything special about the day or event? Will the time of day have any impact? (after lunch meetings require special handling!)

2. How many people will be there? Are they there voluntarily?

3. Will you be inside or outside? How will the room be arranged? Will there be a speaker's platform or lectern? Will you need a microphone? What equipment for visual aids is available?

4. Why are they meeting? What is likely to be the general mood or atmosphere?

5. What is the agenda? Will there be other speakers? What is your placement in the program? What else is happening both before and after your speech?

Note: if you don't have this information, your knees had better be knocking!

If you're reading this, you survived your last adventure in public speaking! Now it's time to analyze your presentation/ speech/meeting . . . .

- How did you feel before you gave the speech?
- What did you do to handle your symptoms of apprehension?
- How well did it work? What will you do next time?
- Assess your use of eye contact.
- Grade yourself on a scale of one to five (five being the best) on the following aspects of making a presentation.

_____ a. Vocal variety

_____ b. Dynamic rate

_____ c. Comfortable pitch

_____ d. Interesting inflections

• Did you assess the audience before hand?

• What did you find out about the audience that you didn't know?

• How did you find out about the speaking situation?

Am I Getting Through?
Making the Message Meaningful

There is no question that Priscilla had a clear purpose in mind when she taught, wrote, or preached the gospel. Her purpose was to inform all who would listen about Jesus Christ and to persuade them to take Him into their own hearts and lives. Her work with Apollos is an example of her ability to craft a message to meet the needs of her audience.

Priscilla opened her home to provide a place for people to worship. When necessary, she traveled to spread the gospel. Her message was all-important, and she worked carefully to be sure it reached an audience. Priscilla is an example to us of a communicator who was committed to helping her audience understand the message of God.

Two Words About Your Message

There are two elements of your message that are critical. It doesn't matter if you are presiding at a meeting, presenting at a seminar, bringing a report at work, or speaking at a women's retreat. These elements—purpose and organization—will "make or break" your effectiveness as a communicator. Let's concentrate now on developing the message. The process is the same whether the message is spoken or written.

Purpose: A clear purpose for any effort you make at communication is critical. If you don't know what you want to accomplish, how can your listener have any hope of getting there with you? The more specifically you state your goal to yourself, the better able you are to plan and develop your communication.

There are five major purposes for a written or spoken piece of communication:

1. To inform—Informing is the cornerstone upon which the other purposes build. You must make the message easy to understand, easy to remember, and easy to use! The goal? A meeting of the minds, a sharing of understanding on the topic at hand.

2. To persuade—Generally, persuasion is designed to convince someone to do or to believe a specific thing. The goal? To move an audience from where they are to a new spot, literally or figuratively.

3. To entertain—Entertainment helps an audience relax and enjoy the experience. The goal? To help the audience escape from reality.

4. To inspire—Inspiring asks for a higher degree of devotion or involvement. The goal? To call the audience to greater enthusiasm and to fulfill the commitments they have made.

5. To call to action—After establishing a need, the solution is presented in the form of action. The goal? To move the audience to immediate, specific action.

```
+-------------------------------------------------------+
|                  Think About This                     |
| Before your next effort at writing or speaking, answer|
| the following questions:                              |
| 1. Why are you doing this?                            |
| 2. Does this communication need to inform, persuade,  |
| entertain, inspire, or call to action?                |
| 3. What is the specific response you hope for from the|
| audience?                                             |
| 4. In one sentence, state the specific purpose of this|
| communication.                                        |
+-------------------------------------------------------+
```

And the second element . . .

Organization: A carefully organized presentation is always easier to remember than one that isn't organized. The side benefit is that it is easier for you, the speaker, to remember as well. You will feel much more comfortable delivering a well-crafted message than a loose, rambling one.

As you put a presentation together, you might want to consider some of the suggestions Carol Kent makes in *Speak Up with Confidence.*

• **Discover an idea**—Ideas are all around you! You may choose an idea based on your knowledge of the audience or to match a theme or even a season. (If your topic has been decided for you, the steps that follow are the same as if you had control over the subject matter.)

• **Determine your aim/purpose**—What matters the most is, did the audience get the speaker's point? If not, their time and yours, as speaker, has been wasted.

• **Gather information**—You cannot shortcut this step! Use libraries, newspapers, reports, etc. as you begin formulating the body of your presentation or speech.

- **Develop an outline**—This step is critical because it will determine your effectiveness as a presenter. Kent says to start with a bang!

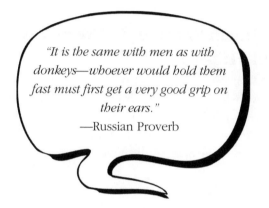

> *"It is the same with men as with donkeys—whoever would hold them fast must first get a very good grip on their ears."*
> —Russian Proverb

Kent says, "Your first twenty-five words should be so well planned that you seize the attention of your audience. Within the first thirty seconds of your talk, the people in the audience have already decided if it's worth their time to listen to you" (Carol Kent, *Speak Up with Confidence*, p. 81).

- **Use good transitional statements**—Use questions, etc. to move the audience to the next point of your outline.

- **Establish rapport with the audience**—This can be done through humor.

- **Use appropriate illustrations**—These can come from personal experience, reading, or research.

- **Application is important**—Look for spiritual applications as you speak or write.

- **Develop a strong conclusion**—Answer the question, *Where do I want to leave the audience?*

- **Pray for God's guidance**—Do this before doing any of the above!

As a Woman Speaker, Is There Anything I Should Know?

Carol Kent believes there are specific guidelines for platform appearance. While she doesn't dwell on attire, she points out that a speaker should find out what the audience will be wearing. It is always fitting to be dressed a bit more formally than your listeners. She gives the following tips especially for women:

- Avoid the "sleeveless" look. No floral, striped, or "cute" dresses.

- Stay away from tight-fitting clothing, see-through materials, skirt slits, etc.

- Be conservative with jewelry. Avoid bangle bracelets or dangle earrings.

- Makeup should bring life to your face but not be "heavy."

- Pay attention to your hair. Does it need a trim?

- Wear stylish but comfortable shoes.

- Carry an attaché case or purse, but never both.

Women of God:
Leaders and Communicators

Abigail, Deborah, Mary of Bethany, Dorcas, and Priscilla were all women who used their talents in the service of God. All were leaders who used their talents. Central to the leadership each demonstrated was her communication skills. From quiet Dorcas to insightful Abigail to impulsive Mary, these women communicated their commitment in their own unique ways.

You also have talents to be used by God. You are a leader in a variety of ways: at home, at work, with friends, in your community, in your church, in your small group, etc. You are always communicating. Everything you do says something about who you are and your relationship to God.

Effective leadership and communication involve skills that must be learned and practiced. They do not happen automatically. Involve others and work together to improve the ways you interact with each other.

My prayer is that this chapter has helped you become more effective in the variety of ways you communicate and lead. You are a woman of God, gifted to serve. May you use your skills and talents in His will!

Chapter Two

Relationship Essentials

By Robert McBride Damon

The Tapestry of Relationships

Who has never felt the need for a friend in a time of crisis or pain? How important that bond is with another person!

Relationship is elemental. We live out our lives within the context of relationships. Beginning with conception in our mother's womb, our very existence depends on the joining of two people who have chosen to be together. Our lives as infants and small children literally depend on the relationships we have with our primary caregivers. As we grow into children, the socialization process begins with playmates and schoolmates. We learn to tolerate. We learn to share. We learn that other people's needs are at least as important as our own. We might not like it, but we find it necessary to give up the infantile idea that the world revolves around us. We discover that we are not the center of the universe after all. What a shock to learn that there are other people to consider.

Over a life span, relationships come to us in multiple sizes and shapes. Each one is like a swatch of fabric that makes up a crazy quilt—triangles, squares, and rectangles. The colors are vivid or muted. The patterns and textures represent an almost infinite variety—stripes, tweeds, plaids, checks, and solids. No two are alike. The threads that stitch them together are the events, experiences, attitudes, and memories that comprise our lives.

Some of our relationships will last forever. Some are of short duration. In some we invest our time and energy and love. In others we maintain emotional distance. An acquaintance is different from a friendship, and a friend can be as close as a sister. The quality of the relationship depends on the depth of our investment.

The best relationships are dynamic. They change over time. Your relationship with your parents changed through your growing-up years. Your parents do not relate to you today as they did when you were a small child. Sometime during the young adult years, the contract between parents and their grown children is renegotiated. Marriages also change over the course of many years. The marital relationship changes from the honeymoon phase, through life's crises, to vintage mellowing. If we are wise, our relationships with our sisters and brothers evolve from childhood rivalry into adult caring and sharing. Friendships are formed and fade, or grow and endure.

The quality of relationships change as the patterns of our lives change. Relationships change by choice or through neglect. They change because we are not the same people at 50 that we were at 20. Relationships change as our needs change. Sometimes they change because something as simple as our address changes. Though we may be nostalgic about the good old days, we cannot go home again, and having left, our relationships may endure, but we are children no longer.

Relationship is the stuff of which life is made. We cannot separate ourselves from it. Our primary relationship is with God in whom we live and move and have our being.

How skilled a pastry maker are you? I watched my mother a thousand times as she mixed pastry dough with her hands. She knew by feel when it was right. She never missed; her piecrust was perfect every time. We have a piecrust relationship with God. All things hold together within that relationship and God never makes a mistake. With God, we have the only perfect relationship we'll ever experience on this earth—no thanks to us. It is God who is the same yesterday, today, and forever (Hebrews 13:8)—gracious, dependable, loving, and forgiving.

Relationship is basic to our existence. Like children, we learn day by day that we are valuable and that others have worth. We learn to get along with people not like ourselves. Our lives are made up of all those who touch us over the years and bring us memories—loving or painful. Each phase of our lives brings new associations. Some old friends move off center stage as new friends move on. We are creatures of change. Sometimes we seek it; sometimes we avoid it. Sometimes it simply goes with the territory as a result of life decisions. Even as we deal with the trauma that change inevitably brings, we find our stability in a relationship with the unchanging God.

This chapter focuses on how women relate to others, why relationships are important to them, and how you as the reader can enrich the relationships you have with your family, friends, coworkers, and fellow believers. Let's do some needlework on this tapestry of relationships and see what designs emerge. No leader can afford to ignore the dimensions interacting relationships have in her own life, nor in the lives of those with whom she works.

Healthy Relationships

A woman went into a bookstore to buy books for her grand-children. She asked the clerk what would be suitable for a four-year-old and a five-year-old. The clerk suggested several children's classics: *The Tales of Peter Rabbit, Winnie the Pooh*, some Dr. Seuss books.

"Those books are old," complained the customer.

"Yes," responded the clerk, "but the children are new."

The child is indeed new. To her, the world is new. As you read these pages, suspend your adult tendencies to critique and analyze. Be aware. Be curious. Be willing to learn. Be just like a "new child."

Words are fascinating. They allow us to conceptualize. Through language, we are able to define ourselves and are able to put our thoughts and concepts into meaningful form. Can we detect any patterns here?

A Look at the Word Relationship

Re-la-tion-ship: the state of being related by kindred, affinity, or another alliance; the mutual exchange between two people or groups who have dealings with one another.

List words that end in the suffix *ship*.

_____ship

_____ship

_____ship

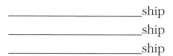

_____ship

_____ship

_____ship

You may have thought of *fellowship, courtship, friendship, partnership, kinship, guardianship, dictatorship, governorship, authorship, readership,* or others. All have to do with relationship.

The suffix *ship* means "ability" or "capability," so that *friendship* means "the ability to be or the capability of being a friend." *Courtship* means "the ability to court." *Worship* literally means "the ability to be of worth."

Re-la-tion-ship means "the ability to relate," to have mutual exchanges. It implies giving and receiving, initiative and respectful distance, mutuality and cooperation. Relationship has to do with "one anothering."

One way we describe various relationships is by using the language of physiology. *Face-to-face* indicates interaction between two people. When we see two people face-to-face, we do not immediately know the nature of the interaction. If we say two people see *eye-to-eye*, we mean that there is agreement in certain matters. If, however, we say two people are *eyeball-to-eyeball*, our impression may be that there is confrontation. Other phrases that describe confrontation or combat are *nose-to-nose, toe-to-toe, hand-to-hand,* or *head-to-head*. The French term *tete-a-tete* is more akin to the English *cheek-to-cheek*, or *arm-in-arm*, which denotes romance. *Heart-to-heart* and *hand-in-hand* are terms that conjure up notions of love, talk, bonding, and friendship. *Mouth-to-mouth* is associated with life-saving resuscitation. *Neck-and-neck* denotes equality and competition. **Note:** As you think about relationships, be aware of the nuances both in definitions and in the reality of the relationships themselves.

In order for you to be an effective leader, you need to understand the characteristics of a healthy relationship. In your leadership role you will be confronted with personality differences, conflict situations, and women who need to

Relationship Essentials

make changes in their relationships. Your success in leadership will depend largely upon on how well you grasp the intricacies of relationship within and outside your place of business, family, community, or church.

On a human level, there is no perfect relationship, but good, solid, healthy relationships *do* exist. Three elements are present in a healthy relationship.

1. Mutuality—A relationship cannot exist within one person. Relationship implies interchanges between or among people. Two people or groups of people either desire or are forced to relate one to another. Two women may choose to be in a friendship. Two other women may be coworkers who find that they are in daily contact and must work together. Whether you find yourself in a friendship by choice, or in a working relationship by chance, mutuality and cooperation are necessary.

2. Initiative—Someone has to make the first move. If you are gregarious, you may find it easy to initiate conversations, plan activities, and do most of the talking and maintenance work on a relationship. If you are more quiet and retiring, this may be difficult to do, as you prefer to wait for the other person to initiate. Since much of life requires interaction, we must all seek to meet each other halfway.

3. Respect—Keeping a respectful distance is a necessary ingredient for any healthy relationship. Being considerate of the other person's personal space is important. There is an invisible line in any relationship that marks the division between what is permissible and what is intolerable. We need to ask permission, wait to be invited, and otherwise be respectful of the rights of other people.

A Look at the Importance of Relationships

Why are relationships so important? They are important because of the benefits we receive from them.

Stimulation. From infancy, we need physical, intellectual, and emotional stimulation. Relationship provides stimulation to our senses and to our sense of well-being. Some people tolerate and need more stimulation in their relationships than others. Outgoing people thrive on movement and activity. Quiet, reserved people might prefer less contact with other people and may have a real need for time alone.

Affirmation. Even the most confident person needs affirmation from others. We develop a sense of self when we see approval reflected in the eyes of someone who affirms us. As we develop our sense of self, we are able to offer emotional support and affirmation to others. A healthy cycle of affirmation begun in infancy can produce healthy adult relationship.

Recognition. If you choose to be in a relationship with me, I feel validated in my sense of worth. I am somebody. Theologically, this is what God does for us in Christ.

Consultation. When decisions need to be made, a "trusted other" can be counted on to listen, evaluate, and advise. Seeing a situation from another perspective gives new insight through information, feedback, and clarification.

Consolation. When life brings pain and loss, family and friends gather to offer consolation and comfort. Emotional support in time of crisis is available through relationships. Giving and receiving consolation happens within relationships.

Realization. Realization is a sense of accomplishment and satisfaction—a job well done. Relationship provides a place to share that realization, which gives it meaning.

Conversation. Listening and talking, understanding and being understood is life- enhancing. Different points of view, different opinions, different outlooks, different experiences— these are designed to enrich our lives.

Communion. The word *communion* literally means "joined together." We are joined together as we converse, and when we are silent we may still be communicating information, feelings, and opinions in a never-ending flow of information to the other.

A Look at Space Issues

In our society there are unspoken but clearly understood distances people maintain in various settings. We begin to relate to another person by the simple act of looking. When the person looks back, eye contact is made and a relationship begins.

Intimate space: Intense activities take place here. Whispers, kisses, hugs, comfort, etc. are given in intimate spaces. People in intimate space are touching or they are relating with very little literal space between them, usually never more than a foot-and-a-half apart.

Interpersonal space: Less intimate conversations occur here between friends. Touch is more limited, and speech takes the form of a normal conversational tone. Distance between people here is between one-and-a-half and four feet.

Social space: More formal interchanges take place in this space. These are typical interactions between business associates, customers with service people, and strangers in conversation. The physical distance here is 4 to 12 feet.

Public space: When your pastor is preaching from the pulpit, his voice is geared to reach a congregation, and while he may have a warm tone, the exchange is not personal. Teachers or politicians who lecture are within the public space. When you call a greeting to a neighbor, you are within the public space. Public space means speaker and listener are more than 12 feet apart.

The setting dictates how we relate to another person. Cultural considerations also come into play. If two North American women friends are conversing, they will sit or stand at a distance that is understood to be comfortable for both. They will look each other in the eyes, and it is permissible for one or the other of them to touch the arm of the person with whom they are talking. If the nationality is changed from North American to Northern European or British, the distance is automatically widened and there will be less touching. If the two women conversing are Latin American or Mediterranean, they will converse more animatedly and the distance between them narrows to inches.

If we take away either of the women and add a man, the whole equation changes. In every culture, when women and men are interacting, there are understood taboos concerning touching, distance, eye contact, and body posture. Contrary to popular opinion, in male/female interaction, men talk more than women do. Men are more likely to interrupt women than they are to interrupt men.

In public, if personal space is invaded by a stranger, people employ distancing tactics to indicate an unwillingness to be engaged in conversation: a closed facial expression, feigned sleep, reading, turning the body slightly away from the other person, staring into space, using earphones. These are clear signals that a person is staking out personal space, even in a crowd.

How Does Relationship Happen?

Sometimes a relationship just happens, such as those from kinship. The quality of a relationship, however, is determined by **intentionality**. Just because you were born of the same parents does not automatically guarantee that you will relate well to each other. An intentional relationship implies a mutual decision, either spoken or by tacit agreement. Two people decide to invest themselves to a degree in their dealings with each other. Relationship may be anything from an acquaintance to a casual friendship to a best friendship. We have acquaintances, friends, close friends, and best friends. Romantic relationships fall into another category altogether.

Geography may determine how much contact you have

with another person, but deep and meaningful relationships often extend over time and distance. In spite of the miles that separate two people, the relationship endures. Frequency of contact has less to do with a relationship than intentionality. A healthy, intentional relationship implies an agreement to relate.

My Friends and Acquaintances

List 1 to 5 persons you consider close to you. Indicate which 2 are the closest.

1.
2.
3.
4.
5.

List your social network. This could be as many as 15–30 persons (including aunts, uncles, cousins, co-workers, church friends, etc.)

You can probably name 100 to 1,000 acquaintances. Name 5 here (the mailman, the man at the supermarket, etc.).

1.
2.
3.
4.
5.

Pause to give thanks for people in your life (in memory, presently, forever) who bring gifts to you. Remember. Feel the joy. Choose one person. Write and send a note of thanks for her contribution to your life.

How Women Relate— Is It Different?

Women are seen as naturally good at relationships. The woman often does the major portion of the maintenance work on a marriage. In female friendships, women tend to talk about personal, intimate matters. With a trustworthy woman friend, they engage in self-disclosure. Female friendships are characterized by mutual understanding and a willingness to be there for the other person.

There has been much debate over gender differences and the possible reasons behind those differences. Some say women are genetically programmed to be what is considered feminine, while others assert they are socialized in ways that produce characteristic results. No one has found a definitive answer, but some interesting observations have been made:

• From infancy, female infants gaze into the eyes of their mothers more than male infants do.

• Girls look each other in the eyes when they converse, while boys tend to look away from each other, avoiding eye contact.

• Adult female friendships thrive on eye-to-eye contact. The same is true of male/female interactions in courtship.

• There seem to be gender differences in the way girls and boys play games and negotiate.

• Women typically take a cooperative stance while working together on projects, but will compete with each other for male attention. Men tend to compete with each other in every area and are often heavily invested in winning.

• Females of all ages are more verbal than males, talking on a more personal level than males.

• Women are much more likely to report having a same-sex best friend than are males.

• Women over 50 tend to identify themselves within their relationships. If asked, "Who are you?" they are most likely to say something like, "I am Mary Johnson, Paul Johnson's wife." Younger women are more likely to identify themselves by what they do vocationally: "I'm Mary Johnson, a computer analyst for Duckworth International."

Stereotypically, women have been negatively characterized as dependent, overly emotional, weak, flirtatious, talkative, shallow, and jealous. Men have been labeled, often unfairly, as cold, distant, unemotional, aggressive, controlling, and ruthless. Both women and men can be any or all of these things. Therefore, women can be:

• selfless yet assertive
• meek yet strong
• modest yet confident
• calm yet effective
• kind yet firm
• flexible yet responsible
• givers yet receivers
• listeners yet talkers
• learners yet teachers

A Look at Labels Women Wear

Such labeling as that above impacts how a woman feels about herself and the relationships she has with others. Issues like equal salary, "pink collar" jobs (nursing, secretarial work, teaching), and "girl talk" are still inflammatory and very controversial. The most important consideration, however, is that as Christian female leaders we must guard against these issues becoming the focus of our lives in leadership. Many are cause for concern and need to be addressed, but within the framework of Scripture and what God intends for us to be doing in His perfect will. We are "labourers together with God," Paul reminds us in 1 Corinthians 3:9 (KJV). Women have discovered, or perhaps they have always known, that whether birthing ideas or babies, the way women work most effectively is together, in a spirit of cooperation—within relationships.

A Woman's Identity: An Inward Look

There is nothing more important than having an identity separate from others. Women have often been lost in the shuffle of conflicting demands. They tend to become the person-of-the-moment based on immediate needs. It is acceptable for bosses, husbands, children, teachers, colleagues, friends, and all others to have needs, but women often feel that it is not acceptable for them to have needs that limit others' access. Many women set no boundaries in order to be of service to everybody and anybody else.

A woman may ask, "Where do I begin and where do others end?" When a woman begins to question and to define herself, she is defining her own identity. An inward look is necessary if we are to lead others to do the same. A working woman needs to look at who she is in order to be a better employee and team member. A community volunteer should know something about her abilities and preferences. A stay-at-home mom will benefit from knowing why she reacts the way she does. A woman in any church leadership position should have a clear understanding of who she is in Christ and what He requires of her.

Let's look at five areas that will help you define yourself by creating a profile of yourself, identifying your likes and dislikes, learning to be assertive, picturing yourself as others see you, and discovering how to relate well to others.

Profiling

Fill in the blanks with the first thought that comes to mind.

1. When I was a child I always wanted to _____
_____

2. My father and I _____
_____

3. My mother and I _____
_____

4. One thing I remember is _____
_____

5. If I could do anything I wanted I would _____
_____

6. One thing that makes me laugh is _____
_____

7. I get angry when _____
_____

8. I am impatient with _____
_____

9. Religion in my life is _____
_____

10. I love _____
_____

11. The thing I most fear is _____

12. I have fun when _____

13. Intimacy is _____

14. I hate _____

15. Something that is important to me is _____

16. I laugh when _____

17. I have the ability to _____

18. One thing I like about me is _____

19. One thing about me I would like to change is _____

20. God is _____

21. My church is _____

What do your answers tell you about the kind of person you are? _____

It is easy to observe the physical changes that take place in people as they progress from stage to stage. Less obvious are the emotional, spiritual, and psychological stages. A healthy person will have good self-knowledge and an idea of how she comes across to others. She will have a sense of her own identity and know how to affirm herself and accept affirmation from others.

Adding Texture

How do you identify yourself? Investigate your self-knowledge by checking the words and phrases that apply to you.

I like:
❑ parties
❑ staring at the ocean
❑ praying wherever I am
❑ many different kinds of people

I feel most comfortable with:
❑ a planned prayertime
❑ people I know well
❑ arriving at appointments early
❑ giving to others
❑ setting and meeting goals for myself
❑ seeking advice before I act

I prefer:
❑ to play things by ear
❑ quiet
❑ meeting new people
❑ organizing an event
❑ doing things myself (being independent)
❑ chairing the committee

I don't like:
❑ unplanned events
❑ a full calendar
❑ a roomful of strangers
❑ to be called on without warning

I find it difficult to tolerate:
❑ someone resting while I'm working
❑ someone working while I'm resting
❑ a messy room
❑ people who won't ask for directions when they are lost
❑ people who squeeze the toothpaste tube in the middle

I react positively to:
❑ punctuality
❑ a relaxed atmosphere
❑ an orderly room
❑ wearing jeans and going barefoot
❑ people who are properly groomed

I have the ability to:
❑ understand how others feel
❑ balance my checkbook
❑ read and fold a map
❑ ask for directions if I'm lost
❑ read people
❑ confront others with their unacceptable behavior
❑ "just know" something without being told
❑ analyze a situation and solve problems

It is difficult for me to:
❑ lose weight
❑ plan ahead
❑ talk to people
❑ be center stage
❑ tolerate laziness

Taken together, the words and phrases you chose give a profile of your values and your preferences.

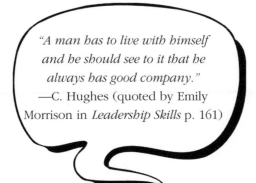

"A man has to live with himself and he should see to it that he always has good company."
—C. Hughes (quoted by Emily Morrison in *Leadership Skills* p. 161)

Your responses to the following questions will provide a fairly accurate picture of who you are and in which directions you need to grow.

1. What do you fear?

People are paralyzed by fears—fear of failure, fear of not

being good enough, fear of loss, fear of abandonment, fear of death, fear to the point of phobia. Fear prevents normal, healthy functioning. The message of the gospel is the antithesis of fear. "Do not be afraid," said the angel to the shepherds (Luke 2:10). "Do not be afraid," said Jesus, walking on the water toward his frightened disciples (Mark 6:50). "My peace I give to you" (John 14:27).

2. What makes you angry?

Do you have a short fuse or a long one? Do you tend to explode or simmer? Do you take your anger out on someone not directly responsible for it? Are you aware of long-term anger you carry? Are you mad at the world? Biologically, anger is nothing more than energy. It is an emotion that people find inconvenient at best and devastating at worst.

Ask yourself, *Do my emotions control me and dictate my behavior, or do I control my emotions?* We cannot help the way we feel; our feelings are valid. We can begin to control the way we think. We can control our behavior. We do have choices.

3. How do you express affection?

Some people are comfortable expressing affection by their actions. Doing kind things is a legitimate way of saying, "I care about you." These are often overlooked or not interpreted as expressions of affection. You may be comfortable with physical expressions of affection. You may, however, be uncomfortable with a verbal or physical expression of love. Physical affection may make you uneasy. Because the expression of affection has become sexualized in our society, people tend to be wary of any expression of affection for fear of being misunderstood or sued.

Gender differences play an important role in our attitudes

toward the expression of affection. Within the marriage relationship, men tend not to separate sexual expression from love, while women tend to believe love and sex are quite different. Obviously, expressing affection for a husband, a friend, a child, or a parent will differ. One of the marks of a healthy, functioning family is the ability to distinguish among these differences.

4. What wounds you?

We are wounded by harsh words, hateful looks, or cold silence, if not by rape, incest, or battering. We are also wounded by caustic humor, sarcasm, or ridicule. Some people are so well defended against pain that they literally cannot feel it. While women have been granted the right to weep, weeping is seen almost universally as a sign of weakness.

5. What makes you laugh?

The benefit of humor in our lives is well documented. We choose our humor style: slapstick, puns, jokes, quirky twists of phrases, etc. Laughter has been called "the saving grace," "internal jogging," and "the best medicine." It is true that when we laugh, our bodies release endorphins into the bloodstream that have a measurable positive effect on our health. It also serves as the lubricant that enhances our relationships. Laughter helps us endure the pain of life. Healthy humor helps us maintain a positive outlook on life. We miss the point if we miss the laughter.

6. What is important to you?

What are your priorities? What do you value? The answers to

these questions give insight into your personality, as moral, ethical, and religious considerations come into play. On a less basic plane, personal tastes and preferences need to be considered.

Being Assertive

One area many women need to explore is their level of assertiveness. Assertiveness has been confused with aggression. Aggression is fueled by the need to control others. Assertiveness is healthy self-confidence.

Adding Texture

Mark each statement true or false.

1. I hesitate to call a friend for fear she may not want to talk to me. ❑ True ❑ False

2. When I have a strong opinion about a subject, I do not hesitate to express myself. ❑ True ❑ False

3. I think of myself as lacking in self-confidence.
❑ True ❑ False

4. If someone does not do a good job, they should be fired and replaced. ❑ True ❑ False

5. I sometimes feel I am not worthy of affirmation from others. ❑ True ❑ False

6. I discipline myself. ❑ True ❑ False

7. I do not like the way I look. ❑ True ❑ False

8. I believe everyone should follow the same rules.
❑ True ❑ False

9. I sometimes feel I have nothing to say that is worth hearing. ❑ True ❑ False

10. I see myself as more often right than wrong.
❑ True ❑ False

11. I sometimes think of myself as stupid.
❑ True ❑ False

12. People should either do their work or get out of the way and let someone else do it. ❑ True ❑ False

13. I believe other people have more to contribute than I do. ❑ True ❑ False

14. I get angry when I have to wait in line. ❑ True ❑ False

15. I am often depressed. ❑ True ❑ False

16. I am often irritable. ❑ True ❑ False

17. I do not want to intrude on others. ❑ True ❑ False

18. I consider myself a person of high energy. ❑ True ❑ False

19. I am often tired. ❑ True ❑ False

20. I believe in "telling it like it is." ❑ True ❑ False

Scoring: Count the number of even-numbered questions you marked true and write the number in the box. Do the same with the odd-numbered.

Even-numbered ☐   Odd-numbered ☐

If you answered true to seven or more odd-numbered statements, you probably need to change the way you think and talk about yourself. Begin to believe you are a worthy and valuable person, created and redeemed by God. Claim the blessings God has for you and confidently become more assertive in your relationships.

If you answered true to seven or more of the even-numbered statements, you probably tend to come across as overly aggressive. Hesitate before you speak, and ask yourself if what you have to say is respectful and kind. Read Galatians 5:22–23 and check the fruits of the Spirit against your behavior.

Picturing Yourself as Others See You

Put yourself in the place of one of your friends. See yourself from her perspective. How would she describe you? What words come to mind? Would she say that you are bright, interested, quiet, angry, cooperative, combative? How do you think you come across to her?

Self-knowledge means knowing what you like, what you are comfortable with, what you are good at (including your spiritual gifts), and how you prefer to do things. It invariably affects the way you relate to other people. You need to be able to name your own strengths and also to recognize those areas in your life that you would like to change. If you know yourself well, you have an idea of how others see you. You can accept yourself as a growing, changing person. You can accept yourself as valued by God and worthy of acceptance by others.

Variety Is the Spice of Life!

What a dull world this would be if everyone were alike! There is infinite variety in the human family. One difference lies in the ways people operate within their relationships. Examine the following contrasts:

• **Some people perceive life in polarities:** black/white, right/wrong, good/bad, win/lose. Others find all kinds of extenuating circumstances and gray areas.

• **Some need time alone** to recoup their energies, to meditate, to rest, to be quiet. Others can't tolerate solitude. They seek out excitement.

• **Some are precise, analytical, and methodical.** Others

are relaxed, unhurried, and comfortable.

- **Some are rule- and policy-oriented.** Others dislike rules and prefer to "play it by ear."
- **Some are visionary dreamers.** Others are practical and down-to-earth doers.
- **Some are tenderhearted and sensitive** to the feelings of others. Others put personal feelings aside and try to be fair.
- **Some want close emotional attachments** and feel abandoned by emotional distance. Others feel suffocated by such closeness.

Each person is unique, of course, but there are some broad categories of personality characteristics.

- **The shy ones:** Shy people are often respectful, apologetic, and self-effacing. At their worst they say: "I have nothing to offer." At their best they say: "I'm a good listener."
- **The independent ones:** These are the people who make a move toward others, but when they feel uncomfortable with too much emotional closeness, they protect themselves by backing away. At their worst they say: "I'll do it my way." At their best they say: "If it's broken, I'll fix it."
- **The warm ones:** These people "come on strong." They are warm and caring, unaware that their affection is sometimes seen as an invasion of personal space. At their worst they say: "Let's have an instant in-depth relationship." At their best they say, "I care about you."
- **The assertive ones:** These may come across too strongly, more aggressive, and confident of their abilities. They are the movers and the shakers, but while they get things done, they are sometimes seen as abrasive or dogmatic. At their worst they say: "I tell it like it is." At their best they say, "The sky's the limit."

Differences in personal style have much to do with how people function within their relationships. Can you see how it affects a leader's approach and the followers' responses?

Which one of the above categories describes you best?
1. shy one
2. independent one
3. warm one
4. assertive one

To which people do you relate best?
1. shy ones
2. independent ones
3. warm ones
4. assertive ones

With which do you have the most difficulty?
1. shy ones
2. independent ones
3. warm ones
4. assertive ones

Which personality would be more likely to assume a leadership role?
1. shy one
2. independent one
3. warm one
4. assertive one

Which personality would have no difficulty cooperating?
1. shy one
2. independent one
3. warm one
4. assertive one

Which personality would get the work done?
1. shy one
2. independent one
3. warm one
4. assertive one

Which personality would be more likely to smooth conflicts?
1. shy one
2. independent one
3. warm one
4. assertive one

As you picture people with differing personal styles in relationships, it enhances your ability to observe and analyze human nature.

Relating Well to Others

Another component in effective relational leading is developing certain techniques or, at the very least, recognizing their value. Learning to relate well is critical to our having the influence we need as leaders of women professionally, in our communities, and in our churches. How can we form healthy relationships?

By recognizing your own value. We are instructed by the apostle Paul not to think of ourselves "more highly than [we] ought" (Romans 12:3). But many women struggle with feelings of worthlessness and have difficulty listing their positive attributes. In order to relate in a healthy way to another person, we need to have a sense of our own worth.

By recognizing the value and worth of others. Everyone has something to teach us. Being receptive and open to different personal styles and views will increase our understanding. Jesus met people where He found them, without judgment and in a spirit of love, regardless of gender, race, social class, or religion.

By having a desire to relate well to others. There are people who prefer not to relate to anyone, those who have withdrawn because of wounding or anger. If we choose to relate to others, we open ourselves to pain. Isolating ourselves from others means we miss the joys life has to offer. Our lives are enriched and enhanced by the positive relationships we form. Relationship requires a conscious choice.

By developing social skills. Such skills include: listening without interrupting, not dominating the conversation, reading and learning in order to contribute to the relationship, and learning to use humor in interactions and knowing when it's appropriate. A consciousness about facial expressions and body language is also important.

By asking for what you need. Often we believe that if others really cared about us, they would know automatically what we need or want. Stating your needs and desires takes the guesswork out of relationships. Women should be careful not to consider everyone else's needs to the neglect of their own legitimate ones. We need to be able to express our desires and needs without being labeled, by ourselves or by others, as selfish.

By being willing to cooperate. Be a part of the team. Taking a cooperative attitude encourages healthy relating.

By learning to sincerely affirm. Everyone likes and needs affirmation. We tend to give affirmation the way we would like to receive affirmation from others. Some people want a hug; others prefer verbal praise. Consider the needs and tastes of others as you seek to affirm.

By leading in your areas of strength and allowing others to lead in theirs. Give yourself permission to express your opinions on subjects about which you have some expertise. Realize that others may differ with you. You can respect their right to believe or react in a manner different from yours.

By learning to set limits. You cannot be all things to all people. It is necessary to draw boundaries around our lives and relationships in order to function well. A healthy relationship does not demand of us more than we can give, and we must be careful not to ask of others more than they can give. Limits must be drawn around three issues:

Time limits: There may be those who will consistently telephone you at three in the morning with a fresh crisis. Obviously, this is a violation of your personhood. Let it be understood that unless someone has a true medical crisis or the house is on fire, it can wait until morning.

Energy limits: There are those who will require all of your energy and will use you to meet their emotional needs. You will find that some people don't bear any part of their own and are happy to unload on you.

Affection limits: Feelings sometimes go awry. If you feel uncomfortable about the level of affection, or the manner in which someone expresses affection toward you, you need to be able to talk to them about it.

Hopefully some of these thoughts and exercises have caused you to know yourself better. While painful at times, this inward look will help you see the design of your unique tapestry—your personality, your abilities, your reactions to different situations. As your life patterns emerge, remember that understanding relationships takes a lifetime!

> *"We steep in the marinade of a fast-paced world. We now expect every-thing to run at the speed of light. Relationships don't operate that way; they need time."*
> —Sandra Crowe (*Since Strangling Isn't an Option*, p. 38)

Let's Take a Trip— Looking Backwards

In case it has escaped your attention, life is not like a cruise where your every whim is met. As we come into adulthood, we carry our baggage with us. All of life's experiences, all of our reactions and attitudes are a part of what we carry. Some-times the burden feels too heavy. Some days it is simply inconvenient and very awkward. What baggage do we carry? Everyone has at least four pieces.

The **steamer trunk** with its curved lid looks like the kind ladies packed with finery when they took a riverboat cruise before the Civil War. Your steamer trunk is uniquely your own and is probably very heavy. You may never have opened it to examine what's inside, or you may have looked and relegated it to the attic.

You carry two very important items inside your trunk: (1) the family rules (written or unwritten) with which you grew up, and (2) your early childhood memories.

Think of the rules your family lived by when you were a child. They may be something as simple as "finish your homework before you watch television." Rules are simply "the way we do things."

Write two rules from your childhood family.

1.

2.

Some rules have to do with money. You may recall that your father was the last of the big spenders. Or your grandmother buried her money under the apple tree. Or your mother worked outside the home and her paycheck was hers and hers alone to spend.

Your family rules shaped and influenced you. You may have grown to adulthood believing that the family rules you grew up with are right. You may not feel comfortable with any deviation from those rules. When we do things for no reason, or because we've always done it that way, there may be a family rule involved. Family rules probably made sense at one time. Some family rules no longer serve their original purpose, but we keep doing things because they are familiar to us.

You may have gone the other direction and vowed, "I'll never treat my children like my father treated me." You may accomplish this, but you are still very much influenced by early family rules. Your need to defy them still gives them power over you.

Your steamer trunk also contains your memories from your early life. They are an important part of the baggage we carry into adulthood.

Picture yourself as a small child before the age of seven. Think of a specific event, remembering colors, clothing, voices, facial expressions, location. Feel the emotions that you felt as that small child.

Write the memory that came to your mind.

How old were you at the time of your memory?

Where did the event take place?

Who was there?

What happened?

What emotions did remembering bring to your mind?

Some people do not remember anything before the age of seven because memories are too painful and are blocked. They are so traumatic that we cannot allow ourselves to remember for fear of re-experiencing the pain, or the event was so trivial that it made no impression. No one gets through childhood without some wounding.

We remember selectively. If you remember mostly warm

and happy events, you may have armed yourself with these good memories and you face the world expecting the best. Your trust level is, very likely, high and your relationships are mostly nurturing.

If you remember only trauma from your early life, you may face the world expecting to be wounded. The world does not disappoint you. Your trust level is probably low and you shield yourself from pain by using any number of defenses. You may cover your pain with bravado, anger, or an I-don't-care attitude. You may find yourself in painful relationships that tend to bring you more pain than joy. It is not that you like being wounded over and over again. It is that it feels very familiar to you—just like home.

What can we do with the steamer trunk? Recognize what's in it—these rules and emotions—and choose the best, refusing to let them continue to have power over you as an adult.

A second piece of baggage you carry into adulthood is the **duffle bag**. In it you carry all the dirty laundry of a lifetime. We are all sinners who have come short of God's glory, but if the gospel has any message at all, it is that we do not have to carry our past sins and failures around with us. "Surely he hath borne our griefs, and carried our sorrows" (Isaiah 53:4*a* KJV). While we know this and read it and other similar verses in the Bible, there is something in us that does not believe that God really will forgive us.

The person who says "I don't deserve to be forgiven" is right on target. God doesn't forgive us because we deserve it. God forgives us because God is love and wants to be in a relationship with us. We sing "Jesus paid it all," but we act as if we must drag the duffle bag of dirty laundry around after us like an anchor weighing us down. There is a release. Come to Jesus for daily cleansing. Do not let the dirty laundry pile up. The great promise of God is that there is grace greater than our sin.

What can we do with the duffle bag? Leave it at the foot of Jesus' cross.

A third piece of baggage we carry is the **backpack**. This is not the kind of backpack that hikers carry with all they will need on a hike. This backpack is filled with anger, animosity, rage, bitterness, and resentment—precisely the things we do not need. It is the kind of baggage that we stuff full to the point of explosion. When someone wrongs us, we add to the contents of our backpack.

Women have the reputation, perhaps undeserved, for never forgetting the wrongs done to them. It is true, however, that some women can, in an argument with a male, say something like: "I'll never forget it. It was July 23, 1973. I was wearing my blue sundress and we were getting ready to go to a family picnic. You said . . . and I said . . . and you answered . . . . I'll never forget it as long as I live."

Why do old resentments simmer? How can we finally be free of the burden of old pain? How can we handle the painful emotions? Anger is not a primary emotion. It covers pain and it covers fear. Many parents teach children that anger is ugly, or worse, that the child is ugly when she is angry. Many of us grew up afraid of adult rage. Now that we are adults, loud voices and angry facial expressions still trigger fear in us.

The Bible teaches that anger in and of itself is not necessarily sinful. Paul's advice to the Ephesians, "Be angry, and do not sin" (Ephesians 4:26 NKJV), is an indication that anger is a human emotion that we will feel. We are warned not to sin because of it. There are three unhealthy ways people handle anger.

1. We dump it. Anger can become a sin when we explode and hurt someone else. When our anger level rises to the danger point, we dump rage on anyone in our path.

2. We deny it. If we feel that anger is a sin, we can smile and deny it to the point that we literally do not feel it. We do not feel anger because we do not allow ourselves to be out of control. Anger does not disappear, however. It will show up somewhere—sometimes as physical symptoms such as headaches, ulcers, or muscle spasms.

3. We turn it inward. Anger turned inward becomes depression. We often have a heavy emotional investment in believing ourselves to be sweet, loving, kind, giving people. In order to maintain that image, we go to great lengths to deny our anger. Holding onto old resentments is self-destructive. We need to learn to let go.

I worked with Jane at a public library years ago. Her husband had died not too long before she was hired as a desk clerk. Jane brought with her several backpacks, all filled with anger! She was angry that her husband left her; she was angry at having to work; she was angry about her life in general. Her inability to let go of her anger resulted in antagonistic behavior toward us as coworkers. It was meted out to library patrons. She had no charitable spirit about any subject and let all of us know how miserable she was. Her weekly trips to the cemetery may well have been times of venting at her husband's grave. The entire time she worked with us she refused to be consoled, to seek counseling, to accept our sympathy. She was comfortable with her anger. It had become part of her and she hugged it to herself tightly.

What can we do with the backpack? Lay it down. Surely there is a better way to live our lives than nursing all the old wounds and inequities. It takes energy to continually deal with all the old wrongs and the resulting anger. Anger can serve as fuel, and its toxic waste spills over onto others, hurting them too.

The last piece of baggage we carry with us is our **flight bag**. As the name implies, it is portable; it goes with us. It is full of our hopes, dreams, expectations, our fantasy of what life will be or should be.

The myths we hold dear go something like this: "I would be happy if I had more money." "I would be happy if I could get my mother (father) to love me." "I would be happy if I found the right person to marry." "Bad things will not happen to me because I am a Christian." We tend to think that if we have Christ in our hearts, we will have happiness. Jesus never promised that. In fact, over the centuries, Christians have suffered because of their faith. Even Christian faith doesn't make all the pain go away.

Life invariably disappoints and wounds because bad things are going to happen. It is a part of the human condition. Some days will be happy, and some days you wonder why you were ever born. Happiness is a by-product of good relationships and productive accomplishments.

What can we do with the flight bag? Scale it down to a manageable size by taking a realistic view of life, and adjust to what you can reasonably expect. Paul said, "I have learned to be content whatever the circumstances" (Philippians 4:11).

Some people go through life asking, "Is this all there is?" and are extremely disappointed. Another person gives up, sighs, and accepts whatever happens as "my lot in life," "my cross to bear." Surely there is middle ground between a head-long pursuit of an unrealistic fantasy and giving up and eating worms! Health lies in knowing who (and Whose) you are, and in productive work and positive relationships. Along this path, you may be surprised by happiness.

Baggage carrying is a universal phenomenon. Some baggage is heavy. Some needs to be thrown overboard. Some of it is useful, and some of it we carry out of habit. Your baggage is unique, yet everyone else in the world can identify with you in the experience. We do not escape the pain of the human condition.

We are unable to get on with our lives as long as we have not examined our baggage. The process is frightening, but we will gain an understanding of who we are. We find courage to face life with God's help. In order to enjoy the patterns and fabrics of our individual tapestries, we must look back before we can move forward and get on with our lives.

Difficult Relationships

Relationships do not always develop in healthy and mutually satisfying directions. When pain, fear, or distrust dominate, the relationship needs to be evaluated and corrective measures implemented.

Think of a relationship that has endured over the years—a friendship, a marriage, or a relationship at work.

Is this relationship nourishing?

1. Does the other person express appreciation for your contribution to the relationship?

2. Does that person express verbal affection to you?

3. Do you sense that the other person enjoys being with you?

4. Do you feel at ease when you are with the other person?

5. Do you believe the other person considers you a positive influence in her/his life?

6. Do you believe there is a realistic balance between the efforts you put into the relationship and the rewards you experience?

Is this relationship toxic?

1. Does the other person often criticize you?

2. Do you find that the other person talks more about your mistakes than your accomplishments?

3. Does the other person frequently lose her/his temper with you?

4. Does the other person yell at you?

5. Does the other person put you down in the presence of others?

Do you recognize the following people?

Everyone knows an **Annabelle**. She is the angry, abrupt,

abrasive, and opinionated woman at work. She does not pick and choose the people she accuses, suspects, wounds, intimidates, and offends. She does it to everyone in her path!

Beverly reacts to Annabelle's behavior by being compliant. She finds herself looking for reasons that explain Annabelle's behavior—she had a difficult childhood, she's feeling ill, or someone was rude to her. Beverly doesn't like doing it, but she feels it is her Christian duty to forgive. She believes the best way to deal with Annabelle is to let her have her way and just suffer through. Being a martyr is not healthy, but she is afraid to act any other way.

What's wrong with this picture?
1. There is no excuse for Annabelle's behavior.
2. Annabelle does not assume responsibility for her own behavior.
3. Beverly has given Annabelle too much power over her life.
4. Allowing Annabelle to have her own way is counterproductive.
5. Fear-based relationships are unhealthy.

Carol also has been offended by Annabelle. Her method of dealing with the situation is to retaliate. If Annabelle needs to control, she is going to get a taste of her own medicine. She is probably the most obnoxious and controlling person ever to set foot on God's green earth. If that's the way Annabelle's going to play, Carol will meet her toe-to-toe. On her better days, Carol knows that her own behavior toward Annabelle is not particularly Christian and sets a poor example at work.

What's wrong with this picture?
1. Carol is caught up in her own anger. She thinks she is in control, but actually Annabelle is.
2. Carol is competing to see who can be more controlling and abrasive.
3. She is aiding and abetting Annabelle in a destructive pattern.

Another coworker, **Diane**, also has been offended and wounded by Annabelle. She has decided to cut Annabelle out of her life. She will be in the same room with her when necessary, but emotionally Diane has opted out. She has withdrawn from the field of battle. Naturally, this creates an intolerable work situation. Diane wonders how a Christian should handle this kind of relationship.

What's wrong with this picture?

1. Christians do not have a right to ignore other people.
2. Diane is engaging in *either/or* thinking—she must either carry Annabelle around as an emotional burden, or withdraw completely.

These scenarios represent three different ways of dealing with the same situation: placate, retaliate, or distance. None is healthy or effective. Each sets up more of the same. The behavior that needs to be changed is instead intensified.

How Do We Deal with the Annabelles?

It is not okay for Annabelle to act the way she does. In spite of her childhood, etc., it is not permissible to treat people the way she treats them. We are accountable and responsible for our own behavior—not that of others, but our own. We cannot help the way we feel, but we *can* begin to change the way we think and control our behavior.

Retaliation is not the way to deal with people like Annabelle. The attitude of *I'll get you for that* is not one that fosters health and peace of mind. Retaliation tends to escalate the conflict, and no one wins.

Distancing is a way of protecting one's self from pain. We distance by being too busy, too tired, or too sick. Diane made a conscious decision in regard to Annabelle. She is saying, *If you need someone in a crisis, don't call me. I do not care.*

Apathy is the ultimate insult. As Christians, we must care.

Does Jesus love Annabelle? Did He die for her? Christian love is not some emotional burden you carry around but the sincere desire that another person will enjoy God's very best.

How to Recognize Inappropriate Behavior

If you have doubts about what is appropriate and what is not, check the following questions.

1. Is it immoral, unethical, or illegal? If you are behaving in any way that breaks the law or violates God's laws, the behavior is inappropriate.

2. Is it manipulative? Manipulation is a form of emotional blackmail. It is behavior that attempts to coerce someone's behavior to suit my agenda.

3. Is it self-serving? People whose goal in life is their own self-aggrandizement set out to have their own way at the expense of others. Most often, if behavior is not for the common good, we may judge it to be inappropriate.

4. Is it malicious? If the intention is to wound, humiliate, frighten, intimidate, or shame another person, the behavior is malicious. Malice can take the form of verbal, emotional, or psychological abuse.

5. Is it out of control? Has the anger turned to rage? Has the indignation become hysterical? Has the telling become overdramatic and histrionic?

6. Is it a misuse of power? Anytime a larger or more powerful person violates the integrity and rights of another and uses size, status, or threats to do so, the behavior is inappropriate. The "larger/smaller" relationship may be boss/employee, parent/child, husband/wife, or two friends. There is a difference between power-grabbing and empowering. Empowering another is an act of healthy relating.

7. Is there turf protecting? Think of someone you know who feels he must protect what he considers his turf. In one tradition-bound group, the women were planning their annual Christmas party. A newcomer suggested a wonderful punch recipe and volunteered to make it. A hush fell. Every woman present turned a shocked face upon her. Someone said in incredulous and reverential tones, "Katie makes the punch." Obviously, the punch was Katie's turf. Giving up our territory and opening ourselves to the ideas and suggestions of others is a choice we make.

8. Is it one up/one down? There are people who cannot feel good about themselves unless someone else is down. Any verbal put-down is designed to put the speaker up. Appropriate behavior dictates equality in value of two people in an interchange, and mutual respectful treatment.

If our individual tapestries and the ones we weave through our relationships are to be healthy, we must repair the frayed edges and mend the broken stitches. As leaders we have to be conscientious in our dealings with others, making sure our service does not stem from hidden agendas, manipulation or intimidation.

How Do We Mend Relationships?

If we desire to be skilled leaders, an important leadership essential is maintaining relationships that are growing in positive directions and of benefit to all involved. Once personalities, background, and experiences enter the picture, it becomes apparent that coping skills will be necessary. There are many such skills we can adopt which will ensure teamwork in our relationships.

Coping Skill #1: How to solve a problem

1. Agree on the definition of the problem.

2. Agree on a time to negotiate.

3. Agree that both parties will remain calm and talk without arguing.

4. Agree on the deadline for solving the problem and a time

extension if necessary.

5. Agree that some things probably won't change. Define these.

6. Agree that solving the problem is more important than holding on to a particular solution.

7. Agree that both are open to new and familiar solutions.

8. Agree that there are resources to help. Define these and appropriate as needed.

9. Solve the problem.

10. Restore the relationship. This can be done by generating some high-energy activity done together, which brings laughter.

Coping Skill #2: Dealing with difficult people

• **Anticipate.** You have dealt with this person before or someone like her/him. What can you expect? Anger? Blame? The silent treatment?

• **Hesitate.** When in doubt, don't. Resist the impulse to speak hot words, be overcome with fear, or ask questions. Pause and gather your wits about you. Unless the person has a gun, pausing will give you a sense of calm!

• **Evaluate.** Ask yourself, *What is the situation? What does this person want? Why is this person acting this way? What are the options? Can I remove myself until the situation calms?*

• **Communicate** forthrightly and in a kind manner. "I have thought it through and I believe . . . I feel . . . I would like . . . I have decided . . . ."

Coping Skill #3: Learning to speak up

Think of someone who has wounded you in the past. It may be a parent, a sibling, a spouse, a friend, a coworker, or a boss. Circle the words that apply.

• When you do not listen to me I feel *dismissed, angry, retaliatory, unimportant.*

• When you withdraw from me I feel *abandoned, rejected, distanced, guilty.*

- When you use sarcasm I feel *diminished, wounded, put down, angry.*
- When you speak harshly in anger I feel *afraid, anxious, devastated, enraged, betrayed.*
- When you give me the silent treatment, I feel *anxious, left out, guilty, powerless.*
- When you blame me or accuse me, I feel *defensive, angry, fearful.*
- When you do not accept responsibility for your own behavior and try to exonerate yourself, I feel *angry, unfairly blamed, accused.*

Coping Skill #4: Learning to let go

Remember an embarrassing incident in your life and then answer these questions:

- When did the event take place?
- Where did it take place?
- Who witnessed it?
- What were the circumstances of the event?
- What words did I speak?
- What did others say?
- What emotions did I feel at the time?
- What emotions do I feel now, recalling the incident?

The baggage mentioned previously in this chapter becomes too heavy to manage when we are unable to let go. Letting go may be turning loose something in our past or it may be letting go of a personal preference in some leadership situation. "Clean Up" states clearly what most of us need to do periodically to enable us to be the type of leaders God can use in His Kingdom's work.

Clean Up

Today I cleaned out drawers and closets.
I threw away an accumulation of bits and pieces,
Odds and ends—
Well, to be truthful, junk—
Faithfully carted from place to place for 20 years.
I tossed a crumbling corsage from the senior prom
Along with brittle, yellow newspaper clippings from
the dim and distant past.
I tossed stacks of term papers and efforts at hand-
work, homework assignments
And old letters.
I threw away photographs—
Of people no one could identify,
Of college friends I haven't seen for 25 years
And very likely never will again,
Blurry ones,
Faded ones,
Six copies of the ones we had seven copies of,
Aunts and uncles and cousins five times removed—
Old clothes and paperback books—
A mountain of trash!
It was cathartic, this clearing out,
And along with the trash I tossed some old dependencies.
Resentments, too, went the way of the trash barrel.
I got rid of a few worn-out ideas, some old regrets,
Old dreams long outgrown,
And two or three outmoded behavior patterns.
I felt as if I'd leaned on the door of my prison cell
Only to have it swing open because it was never
locked.
I felt a lightness,
A freedom,
A release of spirit.
It was a good day—
A most satisfactory day.

Creative Relationships

Throughout history women have been creative needlework-
ers as they have designed and crafted fine tapestries, painting
virtual pictures with silk, cotton, and metallic threads. Just as
they wove and stitched tapestries, they have entered into
relationships of all types. The success of those relationships
was (and still is) determined by one's attitude and skill in
dealing with others. If we are going to be the kind of leaders
who please God, we will have to demonstrate that we know
how to intentionally design creative relationships. Following
are some ideas that might help you show others how to
approach their relationships.

1. I will approach the other person with trust.
2. I will listen to the other person. I will try to hear the
underlying message in what the other person is not saying.
3. I will learn to clarify. I will ask questions and make statements that reframe what the other person is trying to convey.
4. I will not try to defend my viewpoint, point out the truth,
or explain the way it really is.
5. I will draw boundaries. I will not try to change the other
person.
6. I will calmly defend my territory by stating what I will do
in various circumstances. This will be offered without anger
or accusations.
7. I will state my desire to explore options with the other person in order that creative solutions can be found and implemented.

The Ultimate Relationship

Our God is the One who comes to us, the great initiator of relationship. All of Scripture is the story of God's overtures to people. What we know of God is what God has chosen to reveal to us. In the Old Testament, we know about God through creation, mighty acts, personal contact with selected individuals, and through covenant promises, prophets, priests, and kings. The New Testament is the story of God made flesh—God with us. In the fullness of time, God's last and best Word appeared on the human landscape—Emmanuel. There is nothing more significant in all of history than the cross and resurrection event. It was God's gift to us of life, worth, blessing, and hope.

God invites us to be half of a relationship. Revelation 3:20 says, "Behold, I stand at the door and knock. If anyone hears My voice and opens the door, I will come in to him and dine with him, and he with Me" (NKJV).

We are invited to be in relationship with God. We can have daily access to and fellowship with God. Through Christ we are restored into right relationship and are returned to the original blessing of creation.

The nature of the relationship between God and humankind is everlasting. "For I am persuaded that neither death nor life, nor angels nor principalities nor powers, nor things present nor things to come, nor height nor depth, nor any other created thing, shall be able to separate us from the love of God which is in Christ Jesus our Lord" (Romans 8:38–39 NKJV).

Our relationship with God is secure in Christ. Our God is faithful to the promises that we will not be forsaken. Fears come washing over us. We read the newspapers. We live in a violent and unsafe world. We seek safety. We are afraid of being alone. We seek comfort. We have suffered grievous loss. We have suffered betrayal from someone we thought was our friend. Loved ones die and leave us heartsore and stricken by shock and grief. Circumstances conspire to frighten us with the specter of poverty, illness, old age, and death. We cast about to find security. Where is there permanency in a world gone crazy? Only in Christ.

This faithful God who comes to us and brings to us our rooting and our grounding, shows us, in Christ, how to live.

Seeing Ourselves Through God's Eyes

Why should God want to have a relationship with us? Have you ever made a quilt, painted a picture, or designed something? Do you remember the sense of accomplishment and pride you took in that simple act? Imagine how much more God takes pride in the created order. Imagine the pleasure God takes in having relationship with the crown of creation. We can begin to see ourselves, then, as God sees us: worthy and valuable.

It is at the point of our relationships one with another that our faith becomes practical. If faith has worth, it is lived out in our behavior. It is easy to think holy thoughts on Sunday morning but much more difficult to put those thoughts into loving actions Monday through Saturday. Scripture teaches us how to treat each other.

We can take the triune God as our definition of productive relationship. We can know how to relate to God and to each other. The thrust of Scripture deals with the ethical implications of our faith. It dictates the way we are to behave within our relationships. How can we say we love God if we don't love our neighbors, husbands, friends, or supervisors at work? One of the first Bible verses we teach children is, "Be kind one to another." Because God is love, we live in love and behave in loving ways.

Let's Celebrate Relationship!

Women today are making many kinds of choices. They struggle with questions of identity—whether or not to marry, whether or not to bear children, how to support themselves and often their dependents, how to blend career with family responsibilities, how to be safe in an unsafe world.

Women are accomplishing things today that would make our grandmothers either gasp in astonishment or stand up and cheer. And yet, not everything has changed. Wherever there are women, there will be intimate talk. There will be nurturing and caring and laughter. There will be interest in color and texture and beauty. Women will ask each other for advice, for a shoulder to cry on, for a helping hand with the children or with plans for the open house. There will be women who prepare the food and teach the young. Women will be there, just as they were at the foot of the cross and at the tomb on resurrection Sunday, ready to weep, but eager to believe and rejoice. They will do these things in groups or two by two. It is how they do it best—within relationships.

3

Time Management Essentials

By Debbie Lloyd

Me, a Time Manager?

"My clocks are set five minutes fast to help me be on time."

"I never sit down to watch TV unless I have something to do with my hands."

"I enjoy planning my 'strategy of attack' for the day."

"I'm the one who mails Christmas cards as Valentines."

"I'm the one who stays up most of the night before a retreat or program that I've known about for months . . . gathering supplies and preparing notes."

"It's not that I procrastinate, I just try to do too much."

"I'm not really unorganized, I just seem to work better under pressure."

If you can identify with any of these statements, this chapter is for you! Most of us can identify with these women who live out an over-committed schedule. This chapter will deal with establishing priorities, how to deal with interruptions, learning to say no, and making conscious choices about your use of this precious commodity called time.

Take a little time (it will be time well-spent!) to read the following pages. They *could* change your life!

There Isn't Enough Time! Or Is There?

"There is a time for everything, and a season for every activity under heaven."
—Ecclesiastes 3:1

What is time management all about? Is it moving hurriedly and systematically through the day, marking off accomplished tasks from one's list? It must mean more than collapsing into bed at the end of a day holding a crumpled paper filled with affirming check marks . . . marks that chant, "Well done, Busy Bee! Look at all you did today!" Maybe the hurting friend who called really needed more than the recipe. Maybe the secretary in your office needed to talk to someone about her family's shaky financial situation after her uninsured 16-year-old's auto accident.

Time management is more than mechanically squeezing more activities into less time. I've always had the notion that busyness must be related to godliness. Actually, time management may be about doing less, for you see, time management is life management, discerning priorities, having the right perspective, claiming responsibility for our time, accepting interruptions as opportunities, learning when to delegate and when to say no, and feeling good about the choices we have made.

God Is Fair!

Each of us gets 24 hours a day—no more, no less. Each hour is divided into 60 minutes, 3,600 seconds. The difference comes in what we do with our 24 hours. Another person may get more use out of her 3,600 seconds each hour, but she gets not one second more. There is no way to put an extra hour here or an extra day there. We can, however, learn to make the best use of the time we have. When we master our time, we master our lives.

That is what Christian time management is all about. As we begin to listen for and abide by God's plan for our time, we learn to master it, not be mastered by it. The apostle Paul said it well: "Be very careful, then, how you live—not as unwise but as wise, making the most of every opportunity, because the days are evil" (Ephesians 5:15–16).

Make the Time

Look up the following verses. What does the Bible say about time?

Genesis 1:3–5, 14–15

Psalm 74:16

Matthew 25:29

Ephesians 5:15–16

Philippians 4:19

Colossians 4:5

God created time and it belongs to Him, just as our money, talents, and children do. If we acknowledge God's ownership of time, we must also acknowledge that He can stretch it to fit our needs. God will supply all our needs (Philippians 4:19), including time. God doesn't give us a greater number of minutes, but instead helps us use the minutes more efficiently. He increases the quality of what we produce in the amount of time we have.

The Lord's instruction about being a good steward applies to our use of time as well as talents, resources, and money. Paul instructed the early church to "make the best possible use of your time" (Colossians 4:5 Phillips). The Ephesians were charged to use their time wisely and to "make the most of every opportunity you have for doing good" (Ephesians 5:16 TLB). We will also be asked to account for how we spent our time just as the servants in Jesus' parable (Matthew 25:29 TLB).

Profile of the Master Manager

We would be negligent if we did not look at the life of Jesus for some hint as to how to better organize our time. All four Gospel writers present a picture of Jesus under constant pressure, being pursued by friends and enemies, acquaintances and strangers. His every word was monitored, every gesture commented on, every action analyzed. Even so, I never get the feeling that He was rushed, that He had to play "catch up," or that He was taken by surprise. His life showed a wonderful balance, a holy sense of time.

Why Was Jesus Able to Control His Time?

In *Ordering Your Private World*, Gordon MacDonald notes three reasons why Jesus commanded control of His time.

1. He understood His mission—With a key task to perform, He measured His use of time against that sense of mission. Because He had a clear vision of His mission, not even Satan could convince Him to shortcut His Father's eternal priorities.

2. Jesus understood His own limitations and knew the source of His power—Jesus realized that properly budgeting His time would compensate for human weaknesses when spiritual warfare began. Private time, such as the 40 days in the wilderness and the prayer in Gethsemane, were a fixed item on Jesus' time budget. He not only knew His limits; He also knew the source of His strength.

3. Jesus made intentional choices about His time—He invested prime time, taking the disciples through the Scriptures, explaining the deeper meaning of His messages to the crowds. Valuable hours were seized in order to debrief them when they returned from assignments, to rebuke them when they failed, and to affirm them when they succeeded.

Jesus practiced the principle: where your priorities are, there your time will be.

There Is Enough Time!

Jesus was never caught short on time. He knew His mission; He was spiritually sharpened by moments alone with God; and He used wisdom when choosing the focus of His time and energy. At the end of three short years of ministry, He was able to say, "I have finished the work which thou gavest me to do" (John 17:4 KJV). He really is the Master Manager!

To command control of our time we must discover our own purpose as followers of Christ and must establish priorities in line with this purpose. Just as Jesus was spiritually sharpened by moments alone with God, we, too, must budget time for instruction and guidance from the Lord.

First Things First

"But seek first his kingdom and his righteousness, and all these things will be given to you as well."
—Matthew 6:33

In order to gain control of our time, we must clearly understand our mission and measure our use of time against that understanding. To budget our time more effectively, we must first establish priorities within the framework of our life's calling, then set concrete goals to help us live in keeping with those priorities.

Seek the Kingdom First

One of the first steps in becoming a better life manager is to have a clear sense of purpose. What are we to be about as people of God? We are to be His witnesses, to share His love with those about us.

As followers of Christ we quickly claim "Seek ye first the kingdom of God" as a directive for living. But what does this mean? Some may be guided by the thinking, "God first, others second, myself last." We cannot, however, put our lives in compartments. We're not to serve Jesus first, then family, then church, and on down a list. Rather, we are to serve Jesus *as* we serve our family, church, work, community, and our own needs.

This thinking affirms that everything I do is important to God. He is concerned about, and seeks to be a part of, every aspect of my life. This truth relieves much of my guilt about not spending enough time on spiritual things. My personal devotional life and efforts to know God more intimately are vital and deserve deliberate planning. I must seek God all during the day. I must begin my day asking, *How can I seek the kingdom of God today?* and let that question carry me all through the day.

In *The Gift of Time*, William T. McConnell gives a fresh understanding of these instructions from the Lord. McConnell concludes that seeking the kingdom is a basic attitude that defines a Christian's priorities. Reflect on your use of time and determine if seeking the kingdom is a priority for you.

1. To know God

Seeking first the kingdom of God implies the need to set aside time to get to know God, His ways, and His desires. Imagine the relationship that would result from a husband and wife who shared a general commitment but never saw or talked to one another. As seekers after God we must plan into our days times to read and study the Bible, pray, and worship.

2. To take on His character

It is only as we spend time with the Lord that we begin to take on His likeness. What an awesome adventure—to be like Jesus.

3. To serve Him

As we become committed to taking on Christ's character, we will naturally seek to serve Him, follow His teachings, and obey His commands—love others, seek justice, work toward harmony in our world, minister to those in need. This service would include those closest to us, our extended family, those in our Christian community, and the needy in general.

4. To represent Him in every aspect of our life

We are called to represent Christ, to be His spokesmen, to be His incarnation, to continue His work. We are to be bridge builders, connecting others to Him.

5. To bring others to Him

The logical outgrowth of building bridges that connect individuals to God's redemptive love is the growth of the kingdom. This is evangelism . . . providing an opportunity for others to experience the redemptive love of God. Jesus instructed, "*As you go*, make disciples." While you are about your daily tasks, share the good news. This is lifestyle evangelism.

Make the Time

1. Read Luke 18. How does Jesus illustrate the importance of focusing on priorities?

2. What do your consider your number one mission in life?

3. What are some other things that God has called you to do?

4. In what way do (or should) these priorities influence your time schedule?

Adding Hours to Your Day

"Reverence for God adds hours to each day."
—Proverbs 10:27 TLB

The Master Manager not only knew His purpose and mission in life. By His example He taught us the importance of regularly spending time seeking direction and gathering strength to accomplish that mission. Luke's account of Mary and Martha provides a vivid lesson of how we should spend our time. Like Martha, I seem to be so focused on doing good things to please God that I don't take the time for the best, to hear Him, to learn from Him, and to enjoy His presence in my life.

While time management experts may suggest we be like Martha and get more done in less time, Jesus said it was Mary who chose the good thing. When we choose to sit at Jesus' feet, the Martha-tasks more easily fall into place. It is in the daily process of taking the time to sit at the Lord's feet, and in regularly taking time off, that we identify and gain the power to live out our priorities.

Taking Time to Sit at the Lord's Feet

At one point in my life, in my daily devotional time I jumped from one method to another, trying to find just the right one for me, being easily distracted from the task by interruptions and other responsibilities. I also felt guilty when, in my busyness, my quiet time would wane into a time of planning, list making, and organizing my day. Somehow, even through the guilt, the activity seemed to have sort of a sacred effect when first thing in the morning I thought over my day and made lists, schedules, and agendas, and then prayed about the tasks of the day. I knew it wasn't what all the books said to do in a quiet time, but part of it felt right.

While preparing to write this chapter, I had one of those "aha" experiences as I read William McConnell's *The Gift of Time* (now out of print). The author read my mind and expressed my own frustration with my personal quiet time!

McConnell explains that when we read a prepared devotion or a few verses of Scripture out of context, our quiet time is isolated from the concerns of our normal daily activities. He suggests that we make our devotional time more connected with our everyday life. If our personal planning and time management includes space for a quiet time, why shouldn't our quiet time contribute to our planning or time management?

McConnell suggests that if we included a time for planning in our quiet time, we could orient our entire day toward God instead of trying to find a few moments here and there to squeeze Him in. By including planning as a part of our quiet time, four things happen:

1. Our devotions are not separated from the rest of our activities.

2. Our planning can be done in the context of prayer and God's Word.

3. We affirm our commitment to the purpose and values of the kingdom of God.

4. We experience the guidance of the Holy Spirit in establishing our priorities and plans.

Timely Questions

After choosing a Scripture passage (using a devotional book, missions periodical, or prayer guide), read it several times.

• Ask yourself questions that focus your attention on your relationship with God, through thanksgiving and confession. *What am I grateful for? What in the text leads me to thanksgiving? What do I need to confess concerning this text?*

• Ask questions that deal with your response to God in your daily life through intercession and obedience. *How should this passage impact how I pray? What does the Lord require of me here?*

• Ask questions that link your quiet time to how you plan the use of the rest of your time. *What should I do? What should I not do?*

Using this process, our daily to-do list will come out of our time with God. Just as Ananias was instructed to visit Saul (Acts 9:10–19), we may be led to include in our plans things we might have otherwise known nothing about or certainly avoided if we had known. We must remember how different God's ideas of managing the kingdom are from ours. Many times we confuse our own interests with what we think God wants us to do.

Because most of our time is concerned with normal day-to-day responsibilities (families, work, church, civic duties, etc.), thoughts about these "things to do" often intrude into our quiet time. Instead of trying to dismiss these thoughts as secular concerns, sent from the devil to disrupt your spiritual devotion, McConnell suggests that we take time to write them down.

This serves to both free our mind of them and also to help us determine our priorities. In praying about each of these responsibilities, we can get a clearer idea of how each contributes to the kingdom of God.

A quiet time need not be totally private; sharing with someone is an important part of any devotional life. It is essential to share with others who must coordinate their activities with ours.

About That Time Alone . . .

When questions like those in the above exercise become a part of our devotional life, each day becomes linked to other days. Asking these questions provides an opportunity to evaluate our use of time. Why didn't I do what was on my list for yesterday? You may discover you simply had too much to do, or you underestimated how much time a certain activity would take. You may have added activities others could have done, things you thought others expected of you, or things you included hoping God would approve. Your quiet time may also show you that you need to say no more often!

Make the Time

If you are not already committed to a daily devotional time, what steps do you need to take to make this a priority?

How can you incorporate your daily planning into your time at the Lord's feet?

People Are Talking About Time

Time is on our minds, isn't it? We talk about marking time, investing time, saving time, daylight savings time, beating time, and on it goes. We even talk about killing time!

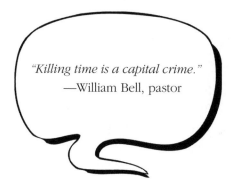

"Killing time is a capital crime."
—William Bell, pastor

Recently while traveling, I found a cartoon in the local newspaper. The drawing was of a crowded cemetery, and on the tombstones were written these epitaphs: "How about 2 weeks from today?" "Call my secretary." "I don't have time for a haircut, let alone death!" "Not a good time." "*Really* not a good time." "Hold my calls." "Give me ten more minutes." "Can't this wait?" "I'm almost finished!" (From *The Honolulu Advertiser*, Thursday, March 11, 2004. Cartoon "Sylvia" by Nicole Hollander, E2.)

These are perfect illustrations of our occupation with time! Perhaps it would be beneficial to look specifically at how we spend our time. Use the following exercise to help you evaluate your use of time.

Make a time log, writing down how you actually spend your time during the day. Every hour or so, write down what you did in the preceding time period. Because the purpose of this exercise is to get the facts out before your memory has a chance to blur them, do not wait until evening to fill in the blanks. Do this for an entire week to get a reasonably accurate picture of your actual time usage. No week is typical; just record your activities and resist the temptation to embellish or tamper with your results.

Another idea . . . break your days into categories. These categories might have to do with relationships, such as time spent with family, friends, coworkers, church family, and yourself. They might have to do with types of tasks, such as professional, home, volunteer, or personal time.

This exercise often helps people recognize illusions about their time usage. For example, you may believe your time is governed by external forces, when in reality you allow your time to be dominated. Some people think they can use their time in any way they wish. However, just the business of living takes up all but a small part of our time. This makes it all the more important to know what we do with our time rather than lose it by default.

After taking one of these time inventories, you may want to make some changes. You will probably *need* to make some changes! As you follow the example of the Master Manager and gain an understanding of your personal mission, you can begin to gain control of your life and your time.

This exercise may prove harder than you think!

Setting Goals for Your Time

Did you think goals were just for other areas of life? Stop and think now . . . .

Once we have acknowledged our Christian purpose, it is important to set goals—to have a plan for life and a strategy of attack. There is nothing like trying to get somewhere without directions; what a real waste of time! "In his heart a man plans his course, but the LORD determines his steps" (Proverbs 16:9).

We get up in the morning, go through the motions, stay very busy, even get tired, but at the end of the day we look back and ask, *What did I accomplish?* We often accomplish so little and waste so much time because we do not know where we are going.

Goals = Direction

The first step in fulfilling our God-given purpose is to establish some directions by setting some precise goals. When it comes to being better managers of our time, goals are essential. As seekers of the kingdom, we all need specific goals to guide us in the use of our time.

Why do goals keep us from wasting time?

1. Goals are motivators

Goals motivate us to take action. Like roadside mile markers, they allow us to see how far we have come and how far we need to go. Goals keep us from wasting time by helping us know what to do next.

2. Goals are tools for decision-making

Goals help us make decisions based not on immediate emotions but rather on sound judgment. Read the account of when Lazarus was ill and how Jesus responded by thoughtfully continuing in His ongoing task and then going to Bethany.

3. Goals are protection from false urgency

It has been said that the important things in life are seldom urgent, and the urgent things are seldom important. The account of Mary and Martha verifies that claim. Martha became a victim of false urgency as she prepared a meal for the Lord while her sister, Mary, focused on the important matter of sitting with the Lord. Often we become victims of the urgent rather than doers of the important.

4. Goals are tools for measuring progress

Goals keep us from wasting time by showing us how far we've come. When there is nothing by which to measure our progress, our time will disappear as mysteriously as money in a poorly managed bank account.

5. Goals are stress reducers

We can see that stress and the achievement of goals are closely related. Focusing on the accomplishments rather than the time involved may reduce stress. By concentrating our efforts toward meeting certain goals, we find personal guidelines and direction, and we can reduce much of the stress of just doing, doing, doing.

More About Goal Setting

It is important to set both long- and short-range goals. By setting and reaching manageable short-range goals, long-range goals become attainable. Goals should include several basic characteristics:

• Worthwhile.

• Specific and measurable (for example, to lose ten pounds by next year).

• Attainable—not so low that they offer no challenge (to lose a pound), but not so high as to be discouraging (to look like Miss America by next week).

• Flexible. Remember, circumstances change and priorities

shift. Don't fail to be sensitive to the need to alter your personal goals.

• Written. This helps you visualize your objectives, strengthen your commitment, and provide a basis for reviewing and checking your progress.

Make the Time

Take time to set some goals for your life, both long-range and short-range in the following areas. Keep in mind that goal setting should be specific, measurable, attainable, scheduled, and flexible.

Physical

Spiritual

Financial

Personal

Relational

Educational

Occupational

Social

A Final Word About Goals

Commit these goals to prayer. Share them with a close friend or your spouse. Mull over them and return to them in several days to revise and polish them. Take note of the benefits of achieving these goals and some of the obstacles you will face in pursuing them. Think about what you need to help you realize these goals. Then, use these goals as the Master Manager did—to help provide direction and structure as you move toward organization of your life and your time.

A Personal Retreat

On several occasions, Jesus withdrew from the crowd, retreating from the busyness of life. Scripture depicts Jesus retreating after busy, people-filled occasions. He knew the value of time alone to regroup, rethink, reevaluate, and refuel. It is also interesting to note that the times after this solitude were always filled with power and the miraculous—Jesus walked on water, calmed the storm, healed a paralytic.

We, too, need time in the mountains. Group worship, private devotional time, and regular Bible study are essential, but sometimes larger chunks of time are necessary to keep from getting bogged down in the details of daily living. A personal retreat gives time to look at the whole picture of one's life and to seek direction from God. Make the effort to set aside retreat time even though it may be very difficult. Schedule it whenever you can. If you cannot set aside the time monthly, consider retreating every other month or quarterly.

Write the date on your calendar, and when the time comes, gather your Bible, hymnal, calendar, notebook, and pen—and leave home. One busy woman insists that leaving home is a must because at home there are too many distractions, such as the telephone and seeing work that needs to be done.

Choose a spot such as the library, a park, the beach, or even your parked car for your retreat. Include these things in your retreat time:

• Find a specific Scripture that you can claim as a promise for the next month.

• Sing or read hymns. There is wonderful doctrine to be found in them!

• Plan the coming month in as much detail as possible—noting personal, children's, spouse's, and family's commitments that concern you. Take stock of wardrobe needs, meal planning, and household and cleaning projects. Try to nail down specific dates whenever possible.

• Bathe all your plans with prayer.

Are You Simply Too Busy for a Retreat with God?

While the temptation is to get more time by cutting out God's share, you will find that the more the day needs stretching, the more time you must spend with God. Martin Luther said, "I have so much to do [today] that I shall spend the first three hours in prayer." I am learning from the example of Jesus that when I spend time with God it enables me to gain greater control over my time and see more clearly what God wants me to do.

Did You Just Say "Take Time Off"?!

The word *leisure* comes from the Latin, *licere*, meaning "to be permitted." We need to give ourselves permission to relax. We would do well to imitate Jesus' example. Following the sixth day of creation, God deliberately stopped working. He took time to relax. No, He wasn't tired. I'm sure He didn't need to recuperate. God set aside time to enjoy His creation. Even with biblical examples to verify the importance of leisure, we still often feel guilty when we take the time to relax.

We need to learn to think of leisure time as something we do for God's purpose. Instead of thinking that we work in order to have leisure, it is more appropriate to realize that we spend time in leisure in order to get on with our work. Modern industry has learned the value of time away from work, thus coffee breaks and mandatory vacations. Any stay-at-home mom knows that she owes her family some time away from the job.

Now hear this! We must assume responsibility for our leisure time! Yes . . . read that again. We must assume responsibility for our leisure time. Rarely will someone else insist that we take it.

Unfortunately, many find that planning for leisure is often more difficult than planning work. If I wait until all my work is done before I sit down to sew (one of my leisurely treats), I grow more and more frustrated because the list never gets completed and I never make it to the sewing machine.

Leisure means different things to different people. My husband enjoys mowing the yard. For me, that is forced labor. My friend Sharon will sit for hours, relaxing with a good book. For me that is *bor-ing*! Leisure for some means going to a movie, entertaining guests, baking bread, going for a walk. Give me half an hour for a refreshing bicycle ride or a dip in the pool!

Sometimes it is best to take leisure as it comes, packaged in various sizes and shapes. It may be an occasional weekend retreat or get-away with a friend, a date with your spouse, or just a bubble bath after the children are finally in bed. Leisure, like gifts, sometimes comes in surprise packages to be ripped into and enjoyed impulsively.

Taking time off for leisure does not mean taking time off from God's plan for our life. Rather, it is refreshing ourselves for the work He has for us to do. We must learn to follow the example of the Master Manager, who regularly took time to pray, to plan, and even to relax. It is in taking the time for a daily quiet time, periodic get-aways for planning and renewal, and regular time-off for leisure and relaxation that we find the needed direction and strength for the journey ahead.

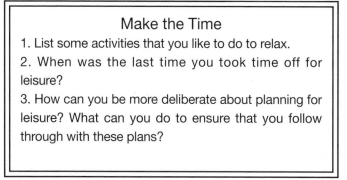

"Your value system greatly affects the way you use your time."
—Emily Morrison in
Leadership Skills, p. 128

Do you ever feel that everyone else has decided how you should spend your time, and you do not have any say-so? These time-consuming activities are the result of a choice—your choice. You did not have to say yes. You made a conscious decision somewhere in the process. We can bring our time under control as we make intentional choices about our use of time and then claim responsibility for the choices we make.

It's All About Choices

I have finally accepted the truth that the Lord will hold me accountable for my use of time just as the servants were responsible for their investment of the master's talents. I will be asked to account for my use of my time, and I want to make sure that I'm the one who decides how I spend it. Too many others have ideas about how I should spend my time! If I have not thought it through and planned the use of my time, then by default someone else will decide for me. Yes, I do have obligations that take up my time. But these obligations are of my choosing, not someone else's.

While many women do not have the option of not working outside the home, choices are still made regarding schedules, overtime, out of town meetings, etc. Women in large numbers comprise an awesome corps of volunteers for community and religious groups. They must realize that the choices they make about their involvement in various activities are ones that affect their families, their churches, and their workplaces.

Because I have chosen marriage and a family, I can accept that keeping the house clean is part of my responsibility. However, I do have choices. I can negotiate tasks with my husband and other family members, hire a maid, be satisfied with a lower standard of housekeeping, or spend most of my time doing housework.

Confessions of a Chauffeur Mom

If you feel that you are spending all your time as a chauffeur service, evaluate the situation. If it is important to you that your children be involved in multiple activities, then accept that this time-crunch is a conscious decision you have made, and make the most of it. If, on the other hand, you feel taken advantage of or resentful, you may need to make a change. Consider limiting extra-curricular activities to a reasonable number, seeking out a carpooling plan with others, or enlisting the help of a spouse or another family member.

Confessions of a Volunteer Leader

I am committed to my personal participation in my own activities and ministries. These obligations and responsibilities didn't just happen. When I accept these choices, I can also accept the consequences—not much "just hangin' around" time, more "quick-fix" and fast-food meals, and lower standards for a clean house. It is not until I accept these decisions and claim responsibility for these choices that I can begin to feel in control of my time.

Don't Skills Count?

Time management skills are not the first step to putting order in our lives. First, we must recognize that time is a gift from God, and that His priorities can always be fulfilled in the amount of time we have been given. Doing God's will does not mean meeting every request that school, church, work, or civic groups propose. Instead, it means knowing what God has and has not called us to do.

Find Time, Take Time, Make Time

We must learn how to invest our time to receive the greatest possible return for the minutes and hours God has given us. Making sound investments of our time calls for disciplined choices. In *Managing Your Life and Your Time* (now out of print), Jo Berry identifies three choices we make when allocating our time: we find time, take time, and make time.

Find-the-time technique. You use this technique when you simply use whatever time is available to do whatever comes along. You agree to serve on the committee at work or church because you have Tuesday night free, not because you feel you have something to contribute or because you are convinced it is God's will for your life. This is a convenient but not very effective time investment method!

Take-the-time technique. This technique requires borrowing time from one task and giving it to another task. People who allocate time this way are already overextended and never ask themselves if they should do something; they just say yes to everything. They rarely accomplish long-range goals because they are doing too much. This is a poor way to invest your time.

Make-the-time technique. This method gives the best return on its investment. Time-makers make time by carefully planning and thoughtfully deciding how to spend unused time. They weigh their opportunities and make choices based on thoughtful preparation.

Make the Time

Take a few minutes to reflect on these questions.

1. In what areas of your life do you feel out of control?

2. In what areas do your responsibilities and time demands seem to snowball?

3. What choices have you made recently that have affected your time demands?

4. Do you need to claim responsibility for these choices so that you can better control your use of time?

5. Are you more of a time-taker, time-finder, or a time-maker? What can you do to be more deliberate about being a time-maker?

Remember . . . The Choice Is Yours!

Once you have made prayerful decisions about your time, accept with confidence the choices you have made and begin to take control of your time. Take the time to evaluate those choices periodically. Realize that your choices will not necessarily be the same as someone else's. There is no need to feel guilty because others have chosen differently. Be willing to accept the decisions that others have made about their time.

Because you are the master of your time and must answer to God for its wise use, it is up to you to take responsibility for the choices you make. You must continually sort through the opportunities available to you and sift out those that do not fit into the life-plan God has shown you. When faced with an overwhelming number of obligations and a limited amount of time, stop and ask yourself, *Is time the problem, or am I the problem?* Then do something about it!

Managing your time is important, but you will never manage your time until you learn to manage yourself.

Walk Wisely

"Be very careful, then, how you live—not as unwise, but as wise, making the most of every opportunity, because the days are evil."
—Ephesians 5:15–16

The Danger of Unseized Time

Gordon MacDonald, in *Ordering Your Private World*, discusses the danger of not being in control of our time. Unseized time is made up of the minutes and hours in our day for which we have not planned. When we haven't thought through our day and scheduled our time, these minutes often get seized by other-than-the-best demands. MacDonald suggests several laws of unseized time, explaining what is likely to happen when we aren't in control of our time.

1. Unseized time flows toward weak areas. We often invest excessive amounts of time doing things we are not good at, while the tasks we are able to do with excellence and effectiveness are preempted.

2. Unseized time is influenced by dominant people in our world. When we do not set up our own time budgets, we find that others force unwanted tasks on us because we have not taken the initiative to command our time.

3. Unseized time surrenders to the demands of all emergencies. As Christian leaders, we must learn that not everything that cries the loudest is the most urgent.

4. Unseized time focuses on things that will bring the most immediate and greatest praise. Instead, we should focus on what is most important and claim our time before everyone and everything else does.

LOST YESTERDAY:
Somewhere between sunrise and sunset, two golden hours, each set with 60 diamond minutes. No reward is offered, for they are gone forever.

—Mrs. Sigourney, taken from old book of quotes

There are several principles of using time wisely that all of us can apply to almost every situation in our busy lives. Whether you are in the workforce full time or part time, or you are a volunteer worker or a stay-at-home mom, these principles will help you organize your time and "walk wisely."

Principle #1: I budget my money. Can I budget my time?

Most of us learned to budget money years ago. When money is limited, we must budget. When time is in limited supply, the same principle holds true. Budgeting your time means determining ahead of time how your time is going to be allotted.

Principle #2: Will planning help?

When I take the time to plan, I have more time. When I stop to think about what needs to be done and my priorities for the day, I approach the day in a more orderly manner. Planning can improve the quality of life, give a sense of direction, and provide a feeling of accomplishment. It develops self-confidence and confirms and strengthens priorities. Surprisingly, planning helps us be more flexible.

There are advantages to planning in the morning, when you are fresh. With the day's priorities clearly in mind, you are less likely to be sidetracked as you go along. Some prefer planning in the evening. Reflecting on what they have done that day helps them select what needs to be done tomorrow.

Besides daily planning, take time at the end of the week to review the week's progress and make general plans for the week to come. My husband and I use Sunday afternoon as planning time. We both spend some time alone, and then we get together to compare calendars, discuss car pool and child-care responsibilities, and negotiate family time.

Principle #3: Why keep a list?

Most everyone makes a to-do list when life gets particularly hectic and the schedule gets tight. The key to finding extra time daily is to make a to-do list every single day. Edward Dayton, in *Tools for Time Management* (now out of print), suggests that making a list accomplishes several things.

- You realize what lies ahead and can set priorities.
- You are able to visualize the tasks ahead of you.
- You are able to cluster related tasks.
- You are free from worrying about remembering what you

need to do.

• You have a sense of accomplishment when you cross items off the list.

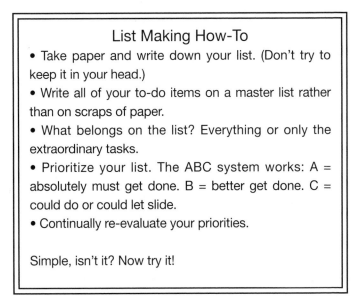

List Making How-To

• Take paper and write down your list. (Don't try to keep it in your head.)

• Write all of your to-do items on a master list rather than on scraps of paper.

• What belongs on the list? Everything or only the extraordinary tasks.

• Prioritize your list. The ABC system works: A = absolutely must get done. B = better get done. C = could do or could let slide.

• Continually re-evaluate your priorities.

Simple, isn't it? Now try it!

Principle #4: How do I get started?

Review your list at the end of the day or the beginning of the next. Add what needs to be added from the old to the new to-do list, and omit those items that can be left undone. Some of yesterday's *B*'s may have become today's *A*'s, but also some became today's *C*'s or can be omitted entirely. Prioritize the new list and begin again, finding satisfaction in completing those priority tasks.

Still reluctant to get started? Don't be tempted to turn to a few short and easy *C*'s, telling yourself that you need a larger block of time for the *A*'s. The problem is, those large blocks of uninterrupted time seldom arise. So go on and start on an *A* task even if you have to spread the task over several small blocks of time.

Take your prioritized to-do list and start assigning tasks in the open slots. Group similar items together, such as errands, phone calls, or correspondence.

Be realistic when you begin to schedule your list. Allow plenty of time to accomplish each task. Be sure to build in "slack time"—a quarter to a third of your day—for unplanned demands on your time. Allow even more than that if you have small children. Don't try to schedule yourself too optimistically or you'll end up feeling frustrated.

Principle #5: Will a weekly schedule really help me?

The key in laying out a weekly schedule is to block out time for those big tasks, tough jobs, or goal-oriented projects. Reserve particular days of the week, such as Tuesday and Thursday mornings, for major projects. Start small by allocating 15 minutes a day to use exclusively for important items.

Try blocking *A* time (for those *A* items) horizontally on a weekly calendar—at the same time each day, Monday through Friday. In "finding" time to write this chapter, I discovered that it was just too easy to find other activities to do. At the end of each day I would say, *Gee I just didn't have much time to write today.* So in order to complete the task I had to block out time. I was finally learning that old planning principle: **there is always enough time for those things that are important to you.**

Principle #6: But I'm different! How do I personalize this scheduling system?

There are numerous systems you can use for scheduling— pocket calendars, day planners, desk or wall calendars, or PDAs. Some calendars are organized by months, weeks, or days; some even have hour-by-hour scheduling. Many computers have programs for designing your own calendar. Palm pilots are useful in this area also. Any of these systems will do four things for you:

1. Provide balance between short- and long-range planning.
2. Provide a record of what has been done as well as what needs to be done.

3. Be accessible to others (family, spouse, work associates) who have need to know what your future commitments are.

4. Be a simple, habit-forming system that does not take too much time to prepare, maintain, or use.

Timely Notes . . .

• Non-essential items crowd into the date book long before the necessities.

• The most important time allocations never seem to scream out immediately when ignored.

• When we neglect our spiritual disciplines here and there, God does not shout loudly about it.

• When we do not allocate time for our family, they generally are understanding and forgiving. If they are neglected too long (when family, rest, and spiritual disciplines are finally noticed), it is often too late to avoid adverse consequences.

• You will "find" a great deal of time by carefully planning whatever you really want to do.

Just like the Master Manager, the busiest people are able to find the time to do what they want to do not because they have any more time than others, but because they think in terms of "making" time by carefully planning, prioritizing, and scheduling.

Make the Time

1. Review the dangers of unsiezed time. To which ones are you most likely to fall prey?

2. Practice planning and prioritizing. Make a list of ten things you must do today. Prioritize your list using the ABC system. Now, try inserting these tasks into an actual schedule.

The Hurrier I Go . . .

Overcommitment is a major time waster. Recall Jesus' words to Martha: "You are worried and upset about many things, but only one thing is needed" (Luke 10:41–42). Jesus reminded us of the danger of trying to do too much. He personally made use of tools for battling overcommitment, including separating the urgent from the important, saying no, and delegating.

Jesus was able to tell the difference between the urgent and the important. When He was told He must go to Bethany because Lazarus was dying, He knew it was more important to continue His present task and go to Bethany later. He discerned the Father's will day by day in a life of prayer, thus warding off the urgent and accomplishing the important. This gave Him a sense of direction, set a steady pace, and enabled Him to do every task God had assigned.

Let's look at how Jesus battled overcommitment.

Separating the Urgent from the Important

As Christians we live in constant tension between the urgent and the important. We are often tempted to let urgent tasks crowd out the most important. Calling for instant action, these demands seem to pressure every hour of every day. We can all recall Christmases where we spent so much energy in preparation that when the day finally arrived we were too exhausted to enjoy it. What teacher hasn't experienced days when she was so involved in the demands of the day that the needs of individual children went unnoticed?

The problem is that the important tasks (prayertime, quality time with my children, a date with my husband, a conversation with that non-Christian friend) rarely call out as loudly as the urgent. Because they can more easily be neglected, we often do not notice the results until it is too late.

How can we decide in our own lives what is important and what is urgent?

• Seek God's guidance as Jesus did.

• Pray for the Lord's direction and wait for His instructions.

• Reflect on your priorities.

• Get an overview picture of how you spend your time by making a personal time inventory.

• Ask yourself, *Will it matter five years from now?*

When faced with a decision about how to spend our time, we must use Christ as our example and separate the important from the urgent.

Saying No

Many lament the fact that they never seem to have enough time. They suffer from a common problem—they can't say *no*. Why is it that one of the first words we learn to say as a child is the hardest word for many of us to say as an adult? When it comes to managing our time, *no* can be the greatest timesaving tool in the English language. We may be saying yes for the wrong reasons when . . .

• we want to gain the approval and acceptance of others

• we are afraid of offending friends and acquaintances

• we feel guilty for not measuring up to someone else's standards

• being busy makes us feel important

• we link overcommitment with spirituality

• we agree because of low self-esteem

• we have a compelling need to be needed by others

Your *Yes* Should Be *No* When . . .

• It leads to overcommitment, which in turn contributes to stress, burnout, and poor health.

• It distracts from our basic objectives.

• It results in the basic purposes of your calling not being fulfilled.

• It leaves you miserable. You find yourself saying, **Why** *did I* *say I would do that?*

• It turns your joy to resentment.

• It means you don't have time to follow through. (Definitely unfair to the other person(s) involved!)

• It robs someone else of a blessing because you took on a project that God intended for someone else.

Before You Say Yes

Unfortunately, people know "yessers" and take full advantage of them! The greater number of talents one possesses, the more essential is the ability to say no. In *Managing Your Life and Your Time*, Jo Berry gives guidelines to follow before you say yes.

Break the *yes* habit. Breaking the habit of saying yes is a basic requirement for learning to say no. Saying yes is easier and more comfortable than saying no. We may be flattered or maybe we want to be liked. We say yes because we dislike confrontation, we don't want to hurt anyone, or we need acceptance.

• Think before saying yes. Evaluate your motives and determine why you are saying yes.

• Prioritize. Pray, asking, *Is it God's will?*

• Investigate. Ask, *What will it cost in terms of time, effort, and progress toward my goals?*

• Consult your calendar, asking how this fits with other plans and responsibilities.

• Make sure others are aware of your time demands. You can't expect friends to know your working hours or schedule if you don't communicate with them.

• Respect your own time as well as others' time. Don't let others establish your priorities. You will be held accountable to the Lord for how you spend your time.

• Don't be a "solve it all." Someone else's time problems are not your responsibility.

You *Can* Say No!

Here are some suggestions of how to say no the right way.

• Don't offer excuses. Do not launch into lengthy explanations. You're not asking for permission to decline; you are saying no.

• Say no with tact and politeness. Be considerate of other people's feelings. Thank the other person for asking you. Provide suggestions, new ideas, or other options if appropriate.

• Develop a method of saying no. Develop a specific *no* statement and practice saying it! Say no clearly, kindly, and inoffensively.

• Stick with the decision you make. Don't give in to the criticism that might result from saying no. Don't feel guilty about saying no. Remember, saying no may be God's will!

The biggest challenge facing Christian leaders is not separating the good from the bad, but taking the best out of all the good. We need to learn that we must say no to some things that we really want to do in order to say yes to the very best things.

Make the Time

Think about some of the relationships or types of situations where you have said yes inappropriately recently.

1. Ask yourself: "What were my motives for saying yes when I knew my answer should be no?"

2. Reflect on an area in your life where you are over-committed. What can you do to correct the situation? Develop and write out a method of saying no. Practice saying it.

Delegating Your Work

Moses is a good example of someone who was filling his time doing good things, yet not accomplishing the God-given tasks before him. It took his father-in-law, Jethro, to point out, "You cannot handle it alone" (Exodus 18:18). This incident sets the classic biblical precedent for delegation as a way of controlling one's time.

Jesus made use of this management skill. When sending out the disciples, He practiced the basic principles of training others. Mark 6 illustrates that Jesus taught and demonstrated what He wanted the disciples to do, sent them out to do it, and provided time for evaluation and encouragement.

Why Don't We Delegate?

• We think that if we don't do it, no one will. I especially find myself thinking this when it comes to church work. I must be like the prophet Elijah, who ran to God saying, "Oh, I'm the only one who cares or is doing anything."

• We have the attitude that no one can do it as well as us. Thinking we are indispensable is a form of false pride that encourages us to waste time.

• We sometimes fear that relinquishing responsibilities means giving up authority or control.

• We may be hesitant to delegate because if someone learns to do the task without our assistance we may not feel needed anymore. What if they can do it better than us? Remember that everyone benefits from the progress of individual team members.

• We believe that delegating is an admission of failure or inadequacy. As we learn to delegate, we are given more time for those relationships and responsibilities that are most important to us.

• We often fear that delegating is an imposition on others who are just as busy as we are. Be willing to carry your part of the load while evaluating the situation. There may be others who could complete the task easier and more efficiently. Don't deny them the blessing of service.

• It takes too much time to delegate. How often have you said, *It's just easier or quicker to do it myself?* This may actually be the case, but training is time well invested.

Make the Time

1. What are reasons you have a hard time delegating?
2. List specific situations where you find it difficult to delegate.
3. Choose one area where you need to delegate. Which of the hints offered in this chapter would be most helpful to you?

Delegating Tips

• Delegate things you can't do.

• Delegate things that others can do better or with greater ease.

• Delegate things that are not a part of your primary goals or tasks. If you aren't personally responsible, delegate.

• Learn to ask for help. Let the need speak for itself. Cut back on the quantity of your work, indicating you need help. Remember, people are not mind readers.

• Make sure the individual understands exactly what you need from her, but don't impose your methods.

• Delegate both responsibility and authority. Don't be guilty of running a one-woman show because you take back what you've delegated. When working with volunteers, giving them responsibilities or the needed authority to step out on their own will give them a sense of ownership.

• Training is a crucial part of delegating. Give all the necessary information, remain available for questions, assist when needed, and offer praise and credit for a job well done.

• Be considerate. Take time to show someone how to do something, then follow up when necessary. When possible, assign tasks that relate to a person's interests and talents and rotate the less pleasant ones.

• Realize that delegating is time-consuming but saves time in the long run. You have to be organized enough to know what needs to be done. It often takes more time to explain, instruct, and follow up than to do a task yourself, but there is a double payoff—both you and the delegatee can benefit. The delegatee learns basic skills, develops talents, and shares ownership in a project. You have time for more important matters.

Confessions of a Procrastinator

As I held the small round wooden piece in my hands, I noticed there were four letters embossed onto its surface: "TUIT" Oh, I get it! Now I had gotten "a round to it!"

Procrastination! Procrastination is defined as the art of post-poning things, putting them off until the last minute, then rushing to finish them and sometimes not getting them done at all. For some, it is the continued avoidance of starting a task and seeing it to its conclusion. For others, it is a matter of doing easier, low-priority chores instead of more difficult, high-priority tasks.

I sometimes wonder if even Paul himself didn't experience similar challenges. He wrote, "I have the desire to do what is good, but I cannot carry it out" (Romans 7:18b). In our efforts to become more like the Master Manager we must gain control of our time by learning to deal with procrastination.

Unfortunately, I'm not known for getting things done ahead of time, and the personal examples of my own procrastination are numerous. As a student, spending sleepless nights finishing papers and cramming for exams at the last minute. Scurrying to take care of last-minute Christmas shopping. Watching the stack of junk in the basement grow to alarming proportions as it awaits spring (ha) cleaning.

My most vivid personal example of procrastination revolves around the birth of my first child, Logan. Early in my pregnancy, a good friend Keri (Mrs. Do-it-ahead-of-time) encouraged me to begin making preparations for the child's birth. Her prodding questions and encouraging suggestions had little effect. I dreamed and planned and shopped but made little concrete effort toward actually getting ready. I guess I wanted the experience of being pregnant, of planning for our first child, and dreaming about the future to last awhile longer.

Well, to make a long story short, Logan arrived while we were vacationing 700 miles from home, two-and-a-half months early. For the next month, as he grew and gained strength in a neonatal intensive care unit, I took care of all of the neglected arrangements . . . announcements, nursery wallpaper and paint, sewing projects. When Logan and I did finally arrive home, four weeks later, he had to sleep in the hall on the floor because the smell of fresh paint was too strong and a bed still hadn't been purchased!

We've All Done It!

Any occasion is an occasion for procrastination—tax time, when the kitchen floor needs waxing, when it's time for routine medical exams. It is human nature to want to avoid things that are difficult, painful, or dull. For some people, procrastination is more than a bad habit. It is an almost paralyzing way of life.

Is a procrastinator lazy? Ornery? Disorganized? Not necessarily.

Jane Burka and Lenora Yuen, authors of *Procrastination: Why You Do It, What to Do About It*, spent the bulk of their professional lives working with chronic procrastinators. They concluded that while one may be tempted to use the above labels, the root of the behavior is often one of several inappropriate fears.

1. Fear of failure

Many procrastinators fear being judged by others or are too hard on themselves. They are afraid they will be found lacking and that even their best efforts won't be good enough.

These people feel their worth depends solely on how well they perform. They do not want to try anything until they know exactly how everything will work. Ironically, when the procrastinator finally moves, there is no hope of doing an outstanding job. By her delay the procrastinator tries to avoid disappointing herself by falling short of her goals.

2. Fear of success

Other procrastinators worry about what will happen if they do manage to do a first-class job. They are rooted in the mistaken notion that success can only bring trouble. Some fear that success might put them in the spotlight where they will be vulnerable to criticism or abuse. Others fear that success might leave them no time to relax. These delayers conclude that, by waiting, they can get the project done in less time and the unused time can be spent for relaxation.

3. Fear of being controlled

Many procrastinate because they want to feel they are in control. It is a way of saying, *You can't make me do this.* In this situation a procrastinator's self-worth is based on her not conforming.

4. Fear of separation

For some, procrastination is a way of maintaining closeness with others. They put things off, do poorly, and ask for endless advice as a way of keeping others attached to them. Some delay in order to maintain a dependent relationship with someone. For example, a divorced woman may procrastinate on all her financial matters because doing it herself means admitting that she is really on her own.

5. Fear of attachment

Procrastination can serve as a means of keeping people at a safe distance, protecting one from intimate relationships. No one wants to get involved with someone whose life seems to always be on the brink of disaster, someone with outstanding debts, a rundown car, a messy house.

6. Other fears

These could be fears of confrontation, the unknown, and facing reality. The Book of Acts gives an account of Governor Felix's procrastination as the result a fearful reaction to Paul: 'That's enough for now! You may leave. When I find it convenient, I will send for you'" (Acts 24:25).

"Today is the tomorrow we worried about yesterday."
—Unknown

Delaying Equations

Are any of these in your life?

Equation #1—Lack of direction = no positive action

Equation #2—No clear plans = no starting point

Equation #3—Spiritualizing decisions = ignoring aspects of God's will that need no translation

Equation #4—Overscheduling = circuit overload!

Equation #5—Failure to prioritize = no motivation for action

Equation #6—Wait-till-the-last-minute lifestyle = possible health issues and strained relationships

Equation #7—Neglect of the important for the urgent = dissatisfaction with accomplishments

Doctor, Is There a Cure?

No, actually there isn't. *But* . . . there are several ways to modify your behavior once you've decided to stop procrastinating. Use the following exercises to help you minimize the round TUIT lifestyle.

• **Analyze your procrastination history.** Write down two or three times when you've procrastinated recently. Describe the circumstances and try to identify the motive. Record the excuses you make. Try to get a clear picture of your particular brand of procrastination.

• **Make a list of all the tasks you tend to put off.** Prioritize that list from the most to the least important. Can some of these tasks be delegated? Can some be dropped or can you trade a task to another person?

• **Set reasonable, specific, concrete, reachable goals.** Break big jobs into manageable chunks, then do them one by one. Describe how you can do this on one of your current projects.

• **Visualize the benefits of completing your project.** Promise yourself a reward and follow through when your goal has been achieved. Don't wait for praise from others (it may never come!), but reward yourself for a job well done. List a reward you're going to give yourself for a task completed.

• **Enlist the support of others as you battle procrastination.** Tell someone what you are working on and when you want to complete it. If you know someone with a goal similar to yours, make a plan together. Call each other for support when you are tempted to quit or need help getting unstuck.

• **Learn to relax.** Learn to be calm when you feel yourself tensing, rushing, panicking. Use scheduled time for leisure and recreation to energize you to action. Write (yes, right now!) some relaxation time into your schedule.

• **Recognize that energy levels vary throughout the day.** If you are a morning person, schedule work on tough, important jobs during your prime time. Schedule easier tasks when you are less attentive. Make a list for tomorrow and schedule according to your energy level.

• **Make an "unschedule" of your already-committed activities.** Procrastinators plan too much, overestimating the time they have available, and underestimating the time it takes to do a job. Make a schedule of daily activities and put in all the things you are already committed to doing or what you think you might be doing. Now look at what uncommitted time you have left. Can you free yourself of some commitments? What changes need to take place to provide more time in your schedule?

• **Use even little bits of time.** Name a project you've never started because you've said you haven't had the full amount of time it will take to complete the project. Now divide it into smaller time blocks. It is amazing how much can be done in a few short bits of time! Try Swiss Cheese!

Poking Holes in Your Projects

Alan Lakein, in *How to Get Control of Your Life and Your Time* (now out of print), suggests using the Swiss Cheese Method to get yourself started on one of those difficult tasks that you keep putting off. By accomplishing several easy five-minute tasks (he calls them *instant tasks*) that are related to the larger project, you have a system of poking holes in the overwhelming job and can gain momentum for really getting started.

It doesn't really matter what instant task you select as long as it's easy (the easier the better) and related to the overwhelming project. The contribution the particular instant task makes is far less important than the overriding objective of the moment: to do something—anything—on the biggie!

In case you aren't positive about whether you are using time to your best advantage, here is a time management tool you can use.

Ask this question: *What is the best use of my time, right now?* Lakein suggests asking yourself this question all through the day.

• Ask it when you complete a task or are at a natural transition.
• Ask it when you have been interrupted by a visitor or a phone call.
• Ask it when you are torn between two different projects.
• Ask it when you notice that you have become distracted.
• Ask it when you detect a tendency to procrastinate.
• Ask it when you are running out of steam.

Put this question on a poster, on a bulletin board, in your notebook, or on your refrigerator as a reminder to keep asking yourself whether you are using your time to your best advantage.

Remember: If you struggle with procrastination, you are not alone!

Through thoughtful analysis of the reasons for our postponing, we can learn how to alter our attitude toward the problem. Changed attitudes become a springboard for modified behavior. We procrastinators with good intentions would do well to adhere to the challenge of Paul in another letter: "Now finish the work, so that your eager willingness to do it may be matched by your completion of it" (2 Corinthians 8:11).

Make the Time

Think about a task that you are facing and apply the suggestions for modifying your procrastination behavior step by step. Write them down.

Redeeming the Time

"All my possessions for a moment of time."
—Alleged last words of Queen Elizabeth I of England

"Walk in wisdom toward them that are without, redeeming the time."
—Colossians 4:5 KJV

Do you ever feel like you are losing time? "Time leaks" are those minutes and seconds we inadvertently let slip from our lives. Like gas leaks in a house, they are difficult to locate and so small they often seem irrelevant. If they aren't traced and stopped, they are costly. Jesus was a master at getting the most out of His time. Just as the early Christians were urged to redeem their time, we too must learn new ways to grab hold of the fleeting moments and make the most of them.

Making Progress While Standing Still

Idle time is when the engine is running but you are actually going nowhere . . . time when the clock is ticking, but nothing is happening. This used to be the most frustrating time for me. I would anxiously flip magazine pages in the waiting room. I would stand in line at the checkout counter, patting my foot as if the constant motion would speed things up. When I saw traffic congestion, I would maneuver around parking lots and store entrances in an effort to not be caught by a light or left waiting in the car.

It was a wonder that I had not contracted some mysterious wrist ailment as a result of constantly checking my watch, watching the precious moments tick by as I stood idly in line or waited impatiently in my car. There must be something to do with those inevitable gaps of inactivity!

Following are several helpful recommendations for making progress during idle time.

• Take something to do when you go somewhere for those just-in-case times—waiting at the doctor's office, arriving early to pick up children from school, etc. Write thank-you notes, hem a skirt, or plan your weekly menu (you do plan menus, don't you?)

• If you have regular idle time, such as commuting, plan ways to use that time. Pray, listen to tapes, plan your day, think through a problem, plan a project. Make those minutes that many consider a waste of time a profitable part of your day.

• Eliminate as much idle time as possible. Call ahead to confirm appointments and to see if you will be seen on schedule. Plan your errands so they can be done on your way to another stop.

• Consolidate your time. Many of us do more than one thing

at a time out of necessity, but often it helps to plan ahead how you might accomplish as much as possible. Make a list of all the things you can do at the same time, then get set up to take advantage of the opportunities.

One word of caution: Be careful not to offend others or devalue precious family time. My husband frequently says to me, "Do you always have to be doing something?" There are times when friends and family members should be given more than my physical presence.

• Keep a list of ten-minute jobs. Post it on a bulletin board. Make a daily list of specific tasks for both home and office. For example:
  • empty the dishwasher
  • clean out a desk drawer
  • update your address book
  • clean off the coffee table
  • sew on a button
  • clean out your purse
  • water the plants
  • make a phone call
  • alphabetize file folders

Make the Time

1. Think about periods of idle time in your day. What can you do to redeem this time?
2. Make a list of standard ten-minute jobs for work and home; post it in a visible place.

Slooow Down!

The old saying that "haste makes waste" is so true. When we hurry, we make mistakes that claim more time than if we had not rushed. It has been said that one of the great disadvantages of hurry is that it takes such a long time.

Have you ever tried to take a shortcut to avoid a traffic problem and ended up getting lost? Burned the cookies because you turned up the temperature to try to cook them a little quicker? How often have you run out the door, late for a meeting, only to return to the house three times to retrieve forgotten items, before you even get down the driveway?

Hurry is counterproductive, decreasing one's efficiency as well as enjoyment. The world is dizzy with hurry, overwhelmed with a desire to precipitate the future. We no longer participate in the simple delights of the earth. How do we keep from hurrying? If you constantly feel rushed, the following suggestions may be helpful.

Pressed for Time?

Did you know you do not have to be busy every minute of the day? Cramming your day with activity is not redeeming the time; rather, it is gulping it down.

Try to savor life, immersing yourself in the simple delights of every day—the morning breeze in your face, moist grass beneath your feet, the smell of honeysuckle in the evening, a child in your arms. Richard Foster in *Celebration of Discipline* has a great deal to say about simplifying life. Check it out at the library or purchase your own copy. You'll be glad you did.

Get a head start. To cover unforeseen interruptions, arrive ten minutes before a scheduled activity. If something unexpected comes up, you can deal with it and still avoid a last-minute rush.

This Program Is Being Interrupted . . .

It never fails. You have 20 minutes to make a 15-minute trip across town for a meeting and your car won't start. You've set the day aside to shop for groceries and run errands and the school calls saying you need to pick up a sick child. Dinner guests are to arrive in 90 minutes and a "long-lost" friend calls for a long chat.

Interruptions! The more you plan and the more focused you seem to be about accomplishing your tasks, the more annoying interruptions can be.

Often, when we take the time to evaluate the nature and frequency of interruptions, we realize that we *can* do something about them. Notice if your interruptions occur regularly or in any sort of pattern—the lonely neighbor calls every morning with some problem or a coworker always stops by your desk to ask your opinion on a project. Perhaps the neighbor doesn't know you're working at home now and the coworker does not understand her assignment.

Frequent interruptions may also signal bad timing on your part. Working on a speech as children are coming home from school is bad timing. Preparing a lesson for a small discussion group in the breakroom at work is bad timing.

"Simple" Interruptions

Which of the following are good techniques for handling interruptions from callers or unexpected guests?

1. Take the direct approach and inform them about your time demands. Yes ___ No ___

2. Say, "Don't call me; I'll call you." Yes ___ No ___

3. Be diplomatic to avoid hurting their feelings. Yes ___ No ___

4. Launch into an involved recitation of your time limitations. Yes ___ No ___

5. Find out what the need is, meet it on the spot, or schedule time to take care of it later. Yes ___ No ___

6. Indicate you want to bring the conversation to a close by looking at your watch every two minutes. Yes ___ No ___

Note: Obviously, 1, 3, and 5, are good ways to let someone know you're busy. The other ways listed are not so good. Appropriate body movements, such as standing or moving toward the door, indicate to your caller that your time is gone. If you regularly find it difficult to close a conversation yourself, ask a spouse, secretary, or coworker to assist by announcing in the presence of the visitor that it is time for your next commitment.

"Divine" Interruptions

There are times when interruptions should be treated as opportunities. Jesus never appeared to be without time for unscheduled interruptions. While on His way to see Jairus' sick daughter, He was interrupted by another person in need . . . not a ruler's child at the point of death, but an unclean, chronically ill woman. He lovingly and patiently took the time to heal the woman and to bless her, turning the interruption into an opportunity.

Charles W. Shedd in *Time for All Things* refers to "divine interruptions." He concludes that one of the marks of Christian greatness is a certain "interruptability." Certainly, the parable of the Good Samaritan is a poignant reminder of a Christian's responsibility to respond redemptively to interruptions.

Timely Tips When You Are Interrupted

Several steps can be taken to deal redemptively with interruptions.
• Shedd suggests disciplining one's self in the art of early starts and before-deadline finishes.
• Look carefully at each interruption, asking God, "What is it You want me to learn from this, or how do You want me to respond to this, Father?"
• Refuse to grow irritable over interruptions.

- Remember that often the interrupter is more important than the interrupted.

A word of caution: Not all interruptions come from God! Some arrive special delivery, designed to discourage and distract. These, too, can be turned into victories, by offering them to God and asking Him to use them.

"Man's interruptions are God's opportunities."
—Old proverb

Make the Time
1. Make a list of your interruptions over the past few days. Do you see any pattern?
2. Recall a "divine" interruption in your life.

The Pinball Syndrome

8:05 A.M. Alone at last. I return to the kitchen, newspaper in hand, for a few solitary moments. I pour a cup of coffee and pop a slice of bread into the toaster. While it is cooking I decide to load the dishwasher. As I go to the table to get my son's cereal bowl I see his Sunday sport coat on the chair. While returning his coat to his room, I decide to take a few minutes to straighten his closet. While there, I pack up a bag of too-small items to deliver to a neighbor. I take them to the kitchen door and there remember my now-cold toast.

I push the toaster button down to quickly rewarm the toast, and while I'm waiting, wipe the counter top. I stop to sort through a stack of mail, and finding a bill that should have been paid yesterday, go to the bedroom to get my purse. On the way, I straighten the pillows on the sofa, stack the newspapers on the coffee table and pick up two pairs of dirty socks. I drop them in the clothes hamper in the bathroom and notice that there is toothpaste all over the sink.

After wiping the sink, I replace the empty toilet paper roll, straighten the towels, and return the baby doll to her appropriate resting place. Stacking a few books on the toy shelf, I notice a dirty juice cup in the corner. Returning it to the kitchen, I see the unpaid bill on the counter, the yet-to-be loaded dishwasher and the cold-again toast. I throw the toast in the garbage and notice that the trashcan needs emptying . . . .

Sound Familiar?

Busy people often suffer from pinball syndrome—bouncing from task to task. We see so many unfinished projects and so many tasks that need to be done that we are easily distracted. Even though we get a lot of little things done, we jump from one task to another and never have a real feeling of completion.

If you stop, however, and take stock, you will see that you really have accomplished quite a bit. Here are some tips for staying focused on our tasks:

1. Have a schedule. Whether you are managing an office, performing household chores, or coordinating a large volunteer event, there is something about establishing a routine that saves everyone time. A schedule keeps you from stopping in the middle of one job to start another that you notice needs doing.

2. Have a system. When you repeat a task over and over in the same way, you both conserve and generate energy. You don't have to waste time deciding how to do something. Develop your own system for doing such tasks as applying makeup, doing laundry, preparing a meal, and handling mail. This is a concrete way to follow the scriptural command to "make the most of every opportunity."

3. Keep it simple. By modifying old habits and eliminating unnecessary steps, you can streamline routine tasks, thus freeing more time for more worthwhile pursuits.

Make the Time

Write down one task you have on a regular basis. Ask the following questions to determine if you can simplify your system:

- Is there a faster way to do this?
- Does this task need doing at all?
- Could someone else do it as well or better?
- Can it be postponed until a better time?

Two "Simple" Habits

You can do a better job of redeeming your time if you will develop two simple habits: simplify your life and get organized.

Simplify Your Life!

"Simplicity sets us free to receive the provision of God as a gift that is not ours to keep and can be freely shared with others."
—Richard Foster, *Celebration of Disciplines*, p. 81

Here are some suggestions for moving toward more clutter-free living.

Before buying anything, ask yourself, *Do I really need this? How often will I use it? What do I already own that I could use instead? Is it worth the space it will take up? Will I have to buy anything else to go with it?*

Go through each room of your house looking for anything that can be thrown away, stored, given away, or put away.

Get Organized!

Because I save everything, most of the time I can't find anything. A good deal of my time goes toward trying to find the item that I put someplace so that I would remember where it was when I started looking for it. I know it's here somewhere.

Organizing helps you make fewer decisions. Putting bills in a special box means never again having to worry about where you put them, or forgetting to pay them. Getting organized ultimately takes less time and energy than dealing with chaos every day. Files, bins, and drawer dividers are inexpensive ways to help find more time for the important things in life.

Make the Time
1. What can you do to simplify your life?
2. In what areas of your life do you need to be more organized?

Who's Doing the Dishes?

Often, in the demands of everyday life, we lose sight of our goals and get sidetracked by things that don't really matter. The urgent demands seem to cry out for our immediate response, and the most important tasks go unattended. When this happens, God's will becomes fuzzy, like a photograph taken with an improperly focused camera.

You are familiar with the story of Mary and Martha, Lazarus' sisters. Let's look again at the scriptural account of one of Jesus' visits to their home, which serves as an illustration for this final discussion on time management.

We Need To . . .

#1: Identify priorities. The story of Mary and Martha provides an excellent example of how easy it is to have a faulty focus on priorities. Martha must have had the gift of hospitality. She was the one responsible for entertaining the guests, for making them feel welcomed. She must have felt that it was a real privilege that the Lord would choose her home to rest and recuperate. Making her guests comfortable was a priority for her.

Her sister, Mary, sat at the Lord's feet listening to what He said while Martha was hustling about. She probably was so attuned to His words that she wasn't even aware of what was going on around her. Martha, on the other hand, became so wrapped up in what she was doing that her activities distracted her from the Lord. Her focus was faulty; her priorities were out of line.

Like many of you, I let the everyday hustle and bustle of life distract me from the Lord. All of us, at one time or another, have become so involved in what we are doing that we forget Who we are doing it for.

The more Martha thought about the situation, the angrier she got and the more self-righteous she felt. Finally, Martha could keep silent no longer. She had to say something! Martha vented her frustration by condemning others who were not as active. She accused Jesus of not caring and before He had a chance to respond, she told Him what to do! She thought she knew better than the Lord or Mary what her sister's priorities should be.

Aren't we a lot like Martha? How often do we take it upon ourselves to tell God what is best for us? We criticize others when actually our own priorities are the ones out of focus.

#2: Limit priorities. Most of us have so many priorities that we're weighted down by the sheer bulk of them. From God's perspective, only a few things in life deserve our intense attention or concern. What a relief! Jesus cautions against overloading our minds and schedules with an excess of unnecessary things. He reminded Martha that everything in life is not of equal significance.

Some things are more important than others. Just as was true for Martha, most of the things we get worked up over aren't that important in the overall scheme of life.

#3: Choose the best. When we place ourselves at Jesus' feet and relinquish our time to Him, He shows us what is necessary and what isn't, and what our personal priorities should be. Knowing our priorities and acting upon them are two different things, however. Notice Jesus' words to Martha: "Mary has chosen what is better" (Luke 10:42). Mary made a choice about how she would spend her time, a choice to focus on her priority.

Many of us are just like Martha was and choose to get sidetracked by the cries of the urgent tasks around us.

Managing our time in a Christlike fashion involves making a series of choices . . . choices about what is important, when to slow down, when to ask for help, when to say yes, and when to say no. You can choose to gain control of your time, just like the Master Manager, as you seek to choose the good things. The choice is yours!

Chapter Four

Group Building Essentials

By Judy Hamlin

Get Going!

*C*ongratulations! You are a leader! The title reflects the confidence others have shown in your ability to accomplish things. When you accept a leadership role, you receive at least two benefits. First, you can feel good about yourself simply because you took the risk and accepted the challenge. Second, being a leader means you have the opportunity to use your skills in your community, family, workplace, and church.

With these benefits come certain responsibilities. Remember, there are no leaders without followers. Those who follow you have certain needs that only you as their leader can meet. Remember, too, that you will be required to learn new skills, improve your expertise in some areas, and simply keep doing your best in other areas. Like it or not, you will become a role model to those who follow you! Never forget this: What you do and how you do it will be perceived by many of your followers as "the way" it should be done.

You'll be faced with many challenges and you'll often have to work with women who lack leadership skills and know little about team building. As you move through this chapter, build from your current level of understanding. Never consider your job done. Take what fits and apply or adapt it. Take your skills and everything you already know, and get going!

—Judy Hamlin

Def-i-nish'-on: gröp

Definition: *group*— "A group is a collection of individuals whose existence as a collection is rewarding to the individuals" (Bernard Bass in K. O. Gangel's book *Team Leadership,* p. 148).

Definition: *group*— "A Christian group can be defined as a gathering of believers with natural interests working towards a common goal" (K. O. Gangel in *Feeding and Leading: A Practical Handbook on Administration in Churches and Christian Organizations,* p. 229).

Leadership means more than showing up to host a meeting, being a project leader, or coordinating an event. It calls for women who will exercise both acquired and God-given skills, and who will develop practical understanding so they can effectively lead those who follow them. Understanding the dynamics of group interaction will help you build a group that functions as it should.

In this chapter, small groups are defined as people with similar interests or needs. Groups exist for a number of reasons and serve a variety of purposes while functioning according to their reasons for existence.

Why Groups Exist

Carl George identifies four primary functions that take place in groups.

• *Loving* indicates sharing, encouraging, and relating positively to one another. Whatever other purposes and functions the group has, love strengthens the group.

• *Learning* includes teaching as well as studying and seeking information. Learning takes place at various stages of group development and involvement.

• *Doing* means putting feet on faith in a variety of ways. The amount of doing the group chooses will be determined by a number of factors—interests, abilities, time allotted, money issues, and available leadership.

• *Maintaining* involves the group's methods of conducting its business—agendas, commitments to common action, and action items.

George uses circles to show how different groups vary in the percentage of time they spend on these four key functions.

A CARING GROUP   A STUDY GROUP   A SERVING GROUP

Examples of group types:

• Caring Group: a support group for widows or divorced women

• Study Group: a women's Bible study group, a long-term specialty training class

• Serving Group: a business/professional Women's club, a missions or ministry group.

Personal Point of View

Choose one of your groups. Divide the circle according to the primary purpose of the group. To determine the other functions, you might ask yourself: *Why was the group formed? What is its main function? Which functions are most important in order for my group to accomplish its purpose?*

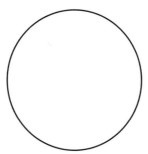

On a separate sheet of paper, draw circle charts for other groups you are involved in or lead.

Why Women Join Groups

Emily Morrison in her book *Leadership Skills* discusses reasons why people—in our case, women—join groups. Something must draw women to participate in this "collection" of individuals. Why? Here are some reasons.

It's okay for her to be there. She doesn't necessarily have to bring influence, power, or money with her. Illustration: Margaret didn't learn to read until she was an adult. You couldn't ask her to read a verse of Scripture without notice. She had no developed skills; she had no understanding of world issues. She had no money to support mission causes. But Margaret did have a willing heart to continue to learn as best she could. She was a prayer warrior, asking when my conferences were so she could be on her knees praying for me. Margaret joined our group because it was okay for her to be there.

She believes in the cause. She can see that the group's purpose aligns with the purposes she has in her own life. That could mean being an advocate for children, equipping other women in life skills, or working in a pregnancy crisis center.

She can have input. Her opinions count; others listen to her. She has a part in the direction of the group.

Her needs are met and the group's activities are of interest to her. She won't join a group where she finds no one her age, nor one that is totally passive in its makeup. If it's a caring group, she'll find encouragement and love. If it's a learning group, she will apply new concepts in her life. If it's a serving group, she'll be involved in those outreach activities.

Why Women Leave Groups

Because women are extremely busy, they may go in and out of groups for a variety of reasons. The following list is especially true for women who volunteer by the thousands to work with children, youth, handicapped, women trying to break the cycle of poverty, and in a myriad of other ministries, both religious and civic.

• They can't see that their participation is making a difference.
• The group's purpose has changed.
• The group isn't (seemingly) concerned about meeting their needs.

- They are not given any opportunity to contribute their creativity or participate in decision-making.
- There are no opportunities for personal growth.

What Makes Members Tick?

Now that we have looked at the group and why it exists and briefly at why women join groups, we need an understanding of the group member. An effective group draws on all members to achieve a goal that cannot be reached by one person. This is true in any group, whether it's a workplace task force, a charitable organization, or a group working on a missions project. Understanding how individuals differ is key to developing an effective group, one that meets needs and reaches its goals.

Meet Suzy, Karen, Marie, and Patsy

In *Welcome to Your First Small Group* (now out of print), I described how four personality types might work together to plan a fellowship dinner. Suzy Sanguine, who is popular, outgoing, talkative, and unpredictable, is the chairperson. Since she realizes she is undisciplined, she enlists Karen Choleric to use her planning and organizing skills to enhance the team. For decorations, Marie Melancholy lends her perfectionist's touch, and Patsy Phlegmatic takes charge on the day of the event, taking care of all the last minute details. Do you see how each personality type contributes to the group?

I will never forget leaving a Christmas missionary dinner with the chairperson of the committee that planned it. The event went very well indeed but in my Choleric mode (can't relax) I felt the need to tell her how I thought we could improve the event the next year. Big mistake!

There is danger in becoming more interested in the subject, program, or event than in people. Don't lose the personal touch. I violated this principle. Virginia, a Choleric/Melancholy who is deep and thoughtful, was quick to point out, "Judy, I would like to reflect and enjoy today. Could we talk about this later?" That hurt, and was a hard lesson for me, but now I am more observant and discerning before speaking my mind.

Spiritual Gifts of Members

Identification of spiritual gifts is also necessary when helping others find their place in ministry. Understand that discovery of spiritual gifts does not equate either to understanding or effective use. People need to know how a spiritual gift relates to their life, to others, to their church, and to the Lord's will for them. Study the New Testament to find descriptions of spiritual gifts, then think of your group members. Books such as *Yours For the Giving* by Barbara Joiner can help you understand gifts from the biblical perspective, and then to realize ways God uses gifted people in His church today.

Growing Group Members

Group members will have various stages of development.

A time of orientation as members get to know and understand one another and become comfortable with their own roles.

A tougher period of negotiation will begin defining member's roles, agendas, and methods of reaching agreement.

Consensus or unity will develop, and the right decisions will result.

How to Be Better Group Members

Morrison discusses the various ways group members can be better participants. These can be applied to any type of group—community task forces, church study groups, ministry projects, neighborhood groups, or teams at work.

• Come to the meeting prepared.

• Arrive on time.

• Stay until the end of the meeting.

• Be attentive, not making lists for the next day or reading a magazine.

• Be perceptive and alert to what is happening.

• Help facilitate discussions. Don't just sit there!

• Be a contributor, either with comments or an interested look on your face. Even nodding your head is good!

• Don't be afraid to disagree. If you don't comment in the meeting, don't take that liberty later.

• Don't be afraid to be creative.

• Give other ideas a fair chance. They might be better than yours!

• Become more tentative—i.e., less certain and/or dogmatic in your views.

Personal Point of View

Make a list of the members of your group. What unique contribution does each person make to the group because of their personality?

Identify the spiritual gifts of 3 group members.

How can you as the leader of the group encourage all members to use their gifts?

What Makes a Group Tick?

The answer to this question is group mechanics—communication, group involvement, and consensus on the group's direction. These elements involve action, participation, and cooperation among all group members. The more good group mechanics are employed, the greater the increase in understanding, retention, involvement, and enjoyment of group members.

Look at the following group mechanics to help you understand your role as group leader, improve your leadership skills, and discover ways to use these components to make your group a success.

#1: Communication—One of the most important processes that takes place in a group is communication.
- In a healthy group, members actively listen to one another.
- To be a good communicator, you must be a good listener.
- Learning to listen is the most basic skill of communication.
- A good listener:
    –allows others to complete their sentences without interrupting.
    –does not silently contradict the speaker.
    –gives the speaker full attention, hearing what the speaker says the first time.
    –is aware of other communication modes besides verbal ones
    –does not given an opinion before it is asked for.
    –looks at the person who is speaking.
- When you are speaking, remember how easily others can miss your point.
- The listener's interpretation of what you say travels through experience and preconceived ideas.
- Make sure you keep your comments simple, repeating if necessary.

As the leader of the group, you have the respnsibility to practice good communication skills. You can, by your example, encourage healthy communication among group members and make it a group characteristic.

#2: Group Involvement—The leader of the group is not the group! All members of a group should be considered and involved whether the group is planning or actually performing its intended function. There are two specific ways to involve the group.

Brainstorming is the first great way to involve group members in the decision-making process. Brainstorming almost always produces effective tools for building the group, and contributes to camaraderie among members.

• **Give** them a topic for discussion.

• **Get** them to write down action ideas on the topic, remembering that no idea or suggestion is wrong.

• **Give** the group an opportunity to share all the ideas.

• **Group** the ideas into categories such as workable, unworkable, and "possibles."

• **Gain** insight through openly discussing each idea. Can any be combined? Can they be amended to work better? Consider factors such as time involvement, cost, and personnel requirements.

• **Guide** the group to select an appropriate number of ideas that show the most potential.

• **Generate** a plan of action for implementing the idea.

• **Go** to other groups as necessary to coordinate projects and activities.

A personal illustration: Our group decided to take a survey to determine whether our meeting times were meeting needs of women within our church. Before taking the survey, we held a brainstorming session of "perceived" problems in getting women to attend functions. This session helped us identify many reasons that were actually given in the survey we did later.

Group activities are a second important element in group involvement as the group accomplishes its purpose. Well-chosen activities will keep the group involved. Use the following guidelines to help you choose and incorporate successful activities into your meetings.

- **Maintain** interest in the activity by starting and ending on time.
- **Make** the directions about the activity clear to everyone.
- **Measure** the amount of time the activity will take.
- **Move** the group from one stage to the next through well-planned and organized activities.
- **Major** on activities that focus on the group's main purpose.
- **Modify** the activity to include every person in the group in some way. (Look for ways to involve those who prefer not to take a visible role)
- **Make** sure members feel that they are important to the rest of the group and feel connected.
- **Maximize** the relevance of the group's activities to the group as well as to its members.

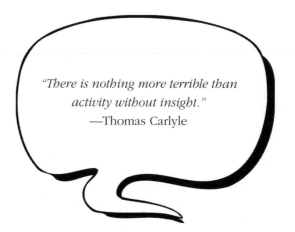

"There is nothing more terrible than activity without insight."
—Thomas Carlyle

#3: Direction of the Group—We have already said that groups need to have a purpose for existing, and group members need to know what that purpose is and what the directions are. Often, when a small group is formed they prepare a formal covenant to guide the group. A covenant will help the group decide on their purpose and goals, and evaluate the results of their group functions.

Preparing a covenant. A good staring point is to identify biblical principles and practices that apply to your group. Members might choose to include guidelines in areas such as prayer, openness, affirmation, availability of group members to one another, and requirements and accountability of group members.

Answering these questions might help you to determine whether or not your group needs a formal covenant:

• **How was your group formed?** If it was formed around a common purpose such as improvement of reading abilities among elementary students, re-assigning office duties, or involvement in a mission project, a covenant can help you determine how members will relate to each other and to the group.

• **What is the common purpose of the group?** A covenant can help members find direction.

• **What goals do group members share?** A covenant can help members define their common goals.

• **What external factors influence the group?** Membership may vary according to the time of the year, current needs, and other factors.

• **How would a covenant benefit your group?** Talk with group members and list reasons for and against the covenant concept. Avoid making it too long, binding, or restrictive.

Your group may not feel the need for a covenant at the beginning, but as the group strengthens and the purpose becomes more clear, you may find you need to clarify your objectives and goals. This can be done with a covenant or at least some type of more formal agreement.

Personal Point of View

Which of these arrows best represents the direction of one of your groups? Which arrow would you choose to represent the group a year from now?

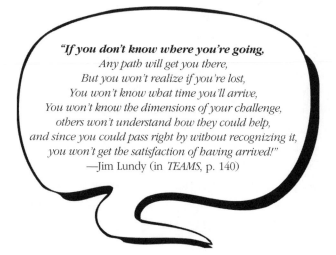

"*If you don't know where you're going,*
Any path will get you there,
But you won't realize if you're lost,
You won't know what time you'll arrive,
You won't know the dimensions of your challenge,
others won't understand how they could help,
and since you could pass right by without recognizing it,
you won't get the satisfaction of having arrived!"
—Jim Lundy (in *TEAMS*, p. 140)

A Few Words About Diversity

Diversity can produce sound consensus decisions, but remember that a diverse group is more difficult to lead. Be prepared to work at developing this leadership skill!

Group make-up diversity: Your group could possibly have members whose first language is not English. Generational differences and background experiences will add to the complexity of your group.

Task diversity: If you are selecting people to work on a task group, choose both task- and relationship-oriented members. The task people will guarantee the job gets done; the relationship people will make sure decisions reflect sensitivity and compassion.

Group size diversity: Task groups should be small, no fewer than 5, no more than 7 members. Even numbers are not desired, as that could result in divided votes. More than 7 members makes it difficult for everyone to contribute.

Growing Groups

Groups naturally go through stages of development. While these stages vary from group to group, some form of developmental process often takes place. Students of group psychology described these stages with various titles. Using Kevin Thompson's explanations from his manual for small group ministry, these stages might be described as:

• The first stage when members look to the leader for help and direction. The leader is not certain about how much freedom to give members.

• A second stage when the leader begins to prepare members to accept more responsibility, and members tend to resist or be anxious about this responsibility.

• The third stage when members try to gain independence and recognition. They often reject the leader, and ignore or contradict the leader's suggestions. The leader needs maturity to accept these attitudes and avoid a power struggle.

• A fourth stage when members gain confidence in themselves, and celebrate by enjoying the group and ignoring the leader. The wise leader will recognize this stage and allow the group to develop and grow.

• A final, productive stage when members accept the leader and are ready to move forward as a productive team. In this stage shared leadership begins to take shape, and often the leader is able to allow the group to move forward on its own.

Who Called This Meeting?

If you are about to begin a group, or plan to begin one at some time in the future, pay special attention to some steps toward making that first decision meeting successful.

1. Begin with prayer.

2. Set an agenda for the meeting and distribute it. Include these items on the agenda:
   • purpose statement
   • goals statement
   • time for members to share their ideas and opinions
   • agreement on goals and objectives
   • voting on decision
   • scheduling future meetings and length

3. Make allowances for differences. Be aware some members will make decisions easily and quickly while others need more information and become anxious if pressed to decide immediately.

4. Keep expectations reasonable. Only so much can be accomplished in this meeting. As a leader, you need to look at what is ideal and what is reality.

5. End on time. At the appropriate time, stop the discussion and summarize the options. If more time is needed, continue if members agree to do so. Provide a graceful exit for those who need to leave. Thank everyone for coming, announce the next meeting date, and close with prayer.

Note: This format can be followed with few adaptations in any workplace, civic, or church group meeting, being sensitive, of course, to parameters regarding opening and closing prayers.

How Did We Do?

Use the checklist below to evaluate your first group meeting.
10–12 checks = successful meeting
7–9 checks = work on areas needing attention for the future
fewer than 7 checks = rethink your agenda and proceedings

___ Started on time
___ Ended on time
___ Atmosphere was non-threatening
___ Discussion allowed everyone to participate
___ Group purpose and goals were agreed upon
___ All points of view were encouraged
___ Questions of judgment were decided by the group
___ Agenda items were brief and clear
___ Proceedings were orderly
___ Unclear statements were clarified
___ Creative thinking resulted
___ Decisions were made and a plan formulated

Meetings may not be a requirement for your group. If the purpose of the group is to perform a specific task, the group may be involved in action that is done outside of a meeting. Most of the same guidelines will apply.

Idea Sampler for Group Building

Members may need to work at developing a group bond. Emily Morrison suggests several ideas to develop a bond between group members. Adapt them for your group.

1. Divide into small buzz groups if group is large enough. If a

small group, read out the following sentences for members to complete.

• As a volunteer, my greatest strength is . . .
• I'm uncomfortable when . . .
• I usually try to make people think I'm . . .
• I love working with people who . . .
• In this group I have felt . . .
• I wish I could . . .

2. Line up the group in the middle of the room and ask them to go to the right for one choice or to the left for the other.

Do you see yourself as . . .

• a leader	or	a follower?
• a luxury car	or	a compact car?
• a rose	or	a wildflower?
• a glass of soda	or	decaffeinated cofee?
• a designer outfit	or	a pair of jeans?
• a sunny day	or	a cozy evening?

3. Paired sharing—take turns sharing with a partner:
• two things you like about yourself
• one skill you feel you have
• one of your most satisfying achievements

Ground Rules for Group Questions

One way to build relationships within a group is by using questions that will help members share with one another. Roberta Hestenes in *Using the Bible in Groups* gives suggestions to help you develop questions that will accomplish group building.

• Think about where your group is now. Focus on the group's past, present, future, affirmation, and accountability as needed.

• Questions should call for information not readily available to other group members, such as: *What is a typical Tuesday*

like for you? What do you like most and like least in your day?
• Ask questions which can be answered briefly in three minutes or less. Remember that three minutes per person, with 10 people, will take at least 30 minutes.

What Kind of Questions Should Be Asked?

• They should be understandable without further explanation.
• They should not require people to give more information about themselves than they feel comfortable doing.
• They should be easily answered by every member of the group.
• They need to be beneficial to other group members as they listen. Some responses might be inappropriate or of no interest to others.
• They need to help the group members to know each other better, enabling them to understand and love each other.
• Avoid questions that call for simple yes/no responses.
• Form questions that have enough variety in response so that all members are not saying the same thing.
• Ask questions that call for personal sharing of the self, not for opinions on issues.
• Be sure the questions can be related to the purpose or focus of the group, rather than tacked-on extras.

More "Ground Rules"

For the use of sharing questions in a group (suggested by Hestenes):
• Allow people to pass if they are not ready to respond. Do check back with them at the end of the sharing time to see if they wish to share now. Don't force them to share.
• Mix questions that call for negative and positive sharing. Don't always ask people to share problems or always to share victories. Mix them up.

- Don't ask follow-up questions after people share unless you intend for only a few to speak. Affirm nonverbally or briefly what has been shared and move on to the next person.
- Usually you ask someone to begin sharing and then go in a circle from there. Begin yourself only if no one else could go first comfortably; if you do begin, be brief.
- Watch the time. If the first one or two members speak at length, intervene by saying, "Let's share briefly so all may have a chance to speak."

Take Me to Your Leader

I've read books on leadership, led leadership training, and taught characteristics of an effective leader, but to me, effective leadership boils down to two basic qualities: compassion (*agape* love) and encouragement. People are looking for leaders who will pray for them, and they are looking for a place to belong, to be significant and accepted. Under your leadership, your group can meet these needs.

The 5 B's of Group Leading

1. Be an Encourager
Jesus modeled encouragement for His followers. He changed Simon's name to Peter, which means rock (John 1:40–42). He referred to Nathanael as "a true Israelite" (John 1:47–51) and Zacchaeus as "son of Abraham" (Luke 19:1–10). He forgave the sinful woman who washed His feet with her tears (Luke 7:36–48).

Bringing out the best in others is perhaps the single most important trait of leadership. As the leader of a group, your skills can be enhanced as you learn and practice the principles of encouragement suggested by Alan Loy McGinnis in *The Friendship Factor.*

• Have high quality and achievement standards. Communicate these to others.

• Be specific when you compliment and encourage others.

• Affirm the good things about others. Publicly acknowledge these good things.

• Reflect on and point out the heroes of our faith—this challenges us to be better followers of Christ.

• Be sincere because people will know whether or you are or not! If they question your motives in this area, they will question them in other areas as well.

If you see yourself as an encourager, you are on your way to becoming a successful leader.

Personal Point of View

Write the names of three people in your group.
Beside those names, write a statement of affirmation.
Look for natural opportunities to verbalize these affirmations.

---

2. Be Decisive

As the leader of a group, opportunities for decisiveness come many times and in many forms. The knowledge that you will surely make mistakes must not paralyze you so that you do not make decisions at all. When wrong decisions are made, the decisive leader analyzes the problem, then looks for a workable solution.

A personal example. One of our major churchwide missions involvement events was our "Back-to-School" dinner and clothing distribution for economically disadvantaged children. One year, a major hurdle appeared. The event had always been in a space that at best would only accommodate 250 people. It became obvious that we were going to attract close to 500 people. While I was away, the group in charge decided, due to tight scheduling issues, to leave the event on the third floor and not move it to our fellowship hall, which could easily handle the increased numbers. The group had acted decisively, but had made what I felt was the wrong decision. I reasoned out why they made such a decision, but reflecting on our goal for this event, I knew that staying on the third floor was not the right decision. When I returned, I met with the group leaders and together we posed and answered a few questions concerning the space issue. We reached a decision by using a member whose moving company transported all the clothing to the fellowship hall before noon. We had a very successful event as well as a good model for identifying and overcoming obstacles. The situation became a demonstration of respect for leadership and success through teamwork, while at the same time maintaining a decisive attitude.

3. Be a Sharer

Sharing leadership is not optional—it's mandatory for accomplishing a mission. One way I demonstrate this principle is to take a plate of cookies to a table of five people and offer a cookie to one, two, three, or four individuals, but never all five. Then after walking away, I ask those who didn't get a cookie how they feel. Responses vary from "left out" and "awkward" to "why me?" Once my point has been made, I give cookies to those who were omitted the first time.

Shared leadership will help a group reach its goals, cut the time it takes to reach them, make the journey more fun, distribute the strength it takes to accomplish goals, and help others feel needed and wanted. Scripture offers many examples and patterns of shared leadership:

King David and his army, Gideon and 300 hand-picked soldiers, Noah and his sons, who built the ark, and Paul, who worked with and through many Christians.

Failure to delegate limits the leader's capacities. Lack of shared leadership is the number one problem causing burnout in leaders. I've tried "going it alone" on major projects, and yes, I've burned out. However, on projects in which I've empowered others to help carry out the goals and dreams, not only did I not burn out—it seemed that before the project was completed, God was giving me another vision. Putting it another way, "What sound does the band make when there's only a band leader?"

Evelyn organized the clothing for the back-to-school event using other volunteers. Mickey headed up the annual church mission fair, which was a massive undertaking. Both women exhibited strong leadership skills and relied heavily on others' assistance. You need people like them because they provide a foundation for expansion of your ministry and free up time for coaching or supporting other volunteers.

Not all situations turn out as positively. Alice accepted responsibility for decorations. She had held the position before and thoroughly enjoyed her work, but her new part-time job meant that she left meetings early, missing fellowship with the other women and the support and appreciation of others. She made it through half the year, then burned out and quit.

4. Be Visionary

Every leader must have a vision and be able to share it with the group. This sharing is critical to the success of the group. How then do we convey our dreams and goals?

• Focus on God's vision.

• Lead the group to compose a mission statement short enough for people to remember and specific enough to describe what you are trying to accomplish.

• Ask questions about the group's purpose and missions work.

- Make certain that members can explain the mission statement.
- Involve everyone in creating a plan to carry out group goals.
- When a goal has been achieved, publicly acknowledge the people involved and stress the importance of the ministry.

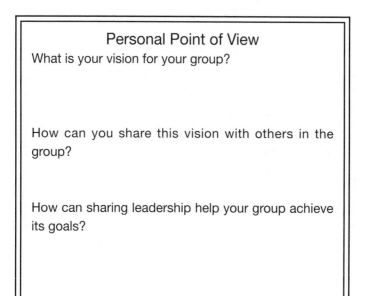

Personal Point of View

What is your vision for your group?

How can you share this vision with others in the group?

How can sharing leadership help your group achieve its goals?

5. Be a Skilled Leader

As the leader, you have the responsibility of keeping the group expectations balanced. If the primary function of your group is *doing*, members will expect to make decisions, plan, and serve—but not spend much time on sharing and other relational activities. If *caring* or *learning* is the primary function of your group, members will expect little business to be conducted but welcome sharing and relationship building time, or time to study.

Jesus modeled group-leading skills for us as He led His disciples. He equipped them to carry on His mission by guiding them as they traveled together, worked together, and learned together.

Leading a group calls for your best in leadership skills.

Discover them
Develop them
Improve them
Use them for His glory

Personal Point of View

Cite biblical examples of ways Jesus:
- was an encourager
- was decisive
- shared leadership
- shared His vision
- demonstrated good leadership skills

You Want Me to Do What?

JoAnn woke up one sunny morning feeling different. She'd gone to bed thinking about the resignation she was going to write, giving up her leadership position of the group of volunteer workers at the Christian Women's Job Corps® site. She was mystified at why she had been unsuccessful at leading this small group of women. But today, she felt okay with everything. Today she was an accomplished, skilled leader . . . .

Wait! This isn't reality. This is a daydream, a fantasy! You will *not* wake up some morning and find a skilled leader inside your body. It doesn't happen that way. Any woman desiring to be an effective leader must develop some skills in how she directs the purposes and activities of the group. The first step in doing this is understanding different leadership approaches and how they relate to group members.

There are no easy answers to the ins and outs of leadership approaches. Roberta Hestenes in *Using the Bible in Groups* uses the following terms to describe how different leaders approach their roles. **No skilled leader will rely on only one approach.** A blended approach will be the most effective. Many use the term "style," but for our purposes, because this term is limiting and gives the idea that it is "one or the other," we are using "approach."

Leadership Approaches

Autocratic (Domineering, dictatorial)
• Total control, with members as listeners and followers.
• Determines goals and policies.
• More interested in subject matter (content) than people (process).
• Makes decisions regardless of other views.
• Talks most of the time.
• Focuses attention on herself.
• Asks and answers all questions.

Authoritative (Definite yet responsive)
• Strong control, with members actively involved in the discussions.
• Has a definite purpose and plan but is open to modification.
• Active and energetic and seeks the activity of others.
• Prepared to give direction and support as needed.
• Uses communication skills to involve others.
• Takes responsibility until others can assume it.
• Uses personal power to empower others.

Democratic (Group-centered)
- Shared control, with leader and members sharing functions.
- Shares leadership responsibility.
- Believes in other people.
- Creates a sense of security and belonging.
- Ensures that others have chance to lead.
- If leader withdraws, group will not fall apart.
- Sees that group discusses all policies.
- May ask others to lead discussion.

Laissez-faire (Permissive, passive)
- Minimal control, with members directing.
- Doesn't prepare and lets things drift.
- Doesn't seem to care.
- Prevents the group from accomplishing anything.
- Encourages fragmentation through lack of discipline.
- Makes no attempt to appraise or regulate events.
- Lacks courage in making decisive plans.

Help Me Practice!

Below are some possible problem scenarios, followed by suggested solutions. Read each and think about a plan of action you might take. Then read the suggested solution that follows at the end of this section. These examples can become guides to help you recognize situations you must deal with, and consider plans of action.

1. A group member begins talking about information that is not on the day's agenda.
2. A group member's behavior disrupts the group meeting.
3. Group members want to "chase rabbits."
4. Group members have blank looks on their faces and no one speaks or asks questions.

Here are my suggested solutions:

1. If you did not have a printed agenda, this is the first step to take in dealing with the problem. You as leader should model the desired behavior, organization, commitment to the project, and attention to detail. If you have emphasized the importance of following an agenda from the start, it will be easier to move the discussion back on track.

2. Meet with that person before or after the meeting to discuss any personal problems that you may not be aware of. Discovering the root of the behavior problem is the first step to take, then prayerfully confront the problem.

3. Remind members of the original purpose of the group/meeting. Use well-planned discussion questions to bring the group back to the project at hand.

4. Perhaps members don't know enough to ask questions. Take time to give background information on a particular ministry, event, mission project, or Bible study, thus facilitating future discussion.

Note: Christian Women's Job Corps® is a national women's ministry for women trying to break the cycle of poverty. For more information and how to get involved in this tremendous ministry opportunity, call 1-800-968-7301.

Personal Point of View

You did so well, let's try several other possible scenarios! My solutions are given afterward.

What would you do if . . .

1. more than half the group members are late or miss the meeting?

2. two group members are carrying on a private conversation during the meeting?

3. members cannot come to a consensus?

4. you don't have enough time to complete the priority items on your agenda?

What Would You Do if . . . Solutions

These are possible solutions to the situations described above.

1. More than half the group members are late or missing?

Begin on time. When it is appropriate, without embarrassing the late-comers, review the agreed start and stop times.

2. Two group members are carrying on a private conversation during the meeting?

Ask one of the talkers a question. If the problem continues, meet with them after the meeting and address the issue.

3. Members cannot come to a consensus?

Have all members had an opportunity to voice their views? Is this an important decision? In the past, have group members been allowed to make decisions? If the answers to these questions are "yes," then take time as a group to list the advantages and disadvantages, then draw a conclusion.

4. You don't have enough time to complete the priority items on your agenda?

If you have not been assigning time limits by each agenda item, start now. If appropriate, assign certain items to a sub-group. With group consent, extend your meeting time.

Remember . . . JoAnn just didn't really wake up one morning a skilled leader, and neither will you! Learning to lead is a process, developed through constant reading, study, and application. Devote some time each day to building your leadership skills.

• Ask your church media center director for leadership skills books

• Look for other leadership resources at your local Christian bookstore

• Take advantage of leadership classes offered in your church or community.

Healthy Group Checkup

Different goals.

Different agendas.

Different purposes.

Different members.

Different perspectives.

It goes without saying that all groups are different. It should also be obvious that some groups are healthy and some unhealthy. Unfortunately, often we overlook or ignore that fact. If we are aware that a group is unhealthy, we often are not sure what to do about the situation, or we avoid dealing with it. First, let's define and compare healthy and unhealthy groups, and then let's examine tools for identifying and improving the unhealthy ones.

Healthy!

Members of a healthy group . . .

- have a feeling of belonging
- enjoy being with one another
- look forward to their times together
- make an effort to attend all meetings
- feel pride in "their" group.

I recall one mission event that required a full day of preparation. Members agreed to work in shifts to get everything together. Some young mothers with small children had to leave when their shifts were up; however, others worked overtime to complete the project. One observer was so overwhelmed with the teamwork that she pitched in to help. The cohesiveness was obvious to even a casual observer.

How does this happen? **Diagnosis:** The leader and all members working together encourage it by including members in decisions, plans, and activities. If a leader or member dominates the group, members will feel less ownership.

Health Hint: Group unity does not mean that there is no conflict.

Preventive Measures—Understand This . . .

✔ Be prepared to handle conflict when it does occur. To be human is to be tempted by self-centeredness, disloyalty, anger, and misunderstandings.

✔ Keep in mind that not all conflict is bad. Disagreements allow people to express their feelings. Being heard by our peers can elevate our self-esteem.

✔ Good conflict is not so difficult to deal with. It's when conflict becomes disruptive and destructive that it becomes difficult. I suggest seven steps for dealing with conflict.

1. Confront conflict when it is small, before it grows into something larger.
2. Try to deal with issues involved, not with personalities.
3. Recognize the feelings and concerns that others have in the situation.
4. Focus on facts of the situation instead of rumors or opinions.
5. Maintain a trusting and friendly attitude with all those involved.
6. Clarify whether one or several issues must be dealt with, and deal with one issue at a time.
7. Assemble all parties in the conflict at one meeting, and reason with all of them at the same time. Pray prior to the meeting!

A personal illustration. I learned the hard way to confront conflict when it is still small. A Bible study group and their leader were experiencing some conflict, but everyone wanted to avoid dealing with the issues. Group leadership soon became another issue. Personal attitudes, lack of prayer, pride, and the fact that the issue had not been addressed when it was small all helped create a much larger problem. Finally, we called a meeting with all parties involved and discussed issues, not personalities. We looked at alternative policy opportunities and temporarily resolved the issue. However, one of the parties in the conflict later resigned.

Rx for a Healthy Group

Healthy groups don't just happen. Some are naturally healthier than others, but like the physical body, a group needs proper nourishment and exercise to maintain its health. As you read these characteristics of healthy groups, you will notice that many are closely related.

Rx—Proper movitation: Members participate because their needs are being met, and they are helping meet the needs of the group. Sustained motivation requires that people know what is expected of them, and usually occurs when members have the opportunity to participate in planning and decision making.

Rx—Wise use of members' gifts: Forget the myth, "give a person a job and he will become active!" Recognize that a person's spiritual gifts, needs, and desires should conform with God's will for them. Within the healthy group no member is called on to use gifts she does not have.

Rx—Respect for the individual: Christian leaders should be people-centered in their approach to the selection and enlistment of group members. People are more important than numbers, methods, or programs.

Rx—Accountability: Members of a healthy group feel accountable to one another, and to the group as a whole. This accountability will affect the way members function in the group, and the way they relate to one another.

Rx—Balance of leader/member involvement: Members of a healthy group share with the leader in the responsibilities and privileges of group involvement. The leader of a healthy group does not do all the leading but delegates some of the tasks, both the pleasant and not-so-pleasant ones.

Rx—Communication: Two-way communication takes place as information is shared. Members aren't left "in the dark," nor do members exclude the leader from the chain of communication.

Rx—Attitude of teamwork: Leaders should emphasize teamwork rather than competition as a group incentive.

Rx—Shared goals: A healthy group is certainly one that is unified in purpose.

Rx—Constructive handling of conflict: Not all conflict comes in the form of verbal disagreements. Some conflict usually exists as different personalities try to blend, and the way the group deals with these personality conflicts determines group health.

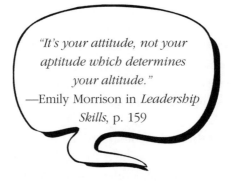

"It's your attitude, not your aptitude which determines your altitude."
—Emily Morrison in *Leadership Skills*, p. 159

Lead, Follow, or Get Out of the Way!

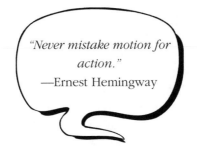

"Never mistake motion for action."
—Ernest Hemingway

Myth: Some groups are perfect.
Truth: Groups, like people, are not perfect, and never will be. They are made up of imperfect members, and have imperfect leaders. There are common pitfalls in group dynamics that can be avoided, or at least dealt with when they occur.

Myth: A leader is stuck with a group's behavior and can't change it.

Truth: By being aware of potential problems and by learning skills that will help in solving these problems, the leader can guide members to become a healthy, functioning group. The leader sets the tone for most participant behavior.

Myth: The reason for most groups' problems is a lack of vision.

Truth: A fundamental reason for the majority of our problems is ineffective communication, both with one another and with God. We should always be mindful of the instructions of Proverbs 19:21: "Many are the plans in a man's heart, but it is the LORD's purpose that prevails." Prayer is our communication with God; make it a daily part of your leadership preparation.

Potential Pitfalls

Problems for groups usually appear in four basic areas: 1. problems related to the basics of the meetings of the group; 2. problems with leadership skills; 3. faulty administrative functions; 4. poor participant behaviors.

As you read the list below, next to each statement write the number of the problem area that you feel is appropriate for the statement. For example, a group that is too large has the potential of problems in all four areas: there is a problem with the meeting; leadership needs to deal with the problem; administrative actions could relieve the problem; participant behavior is affected.

Group is too large
Location of meetings is inconvenient
Seating arrangement is inappropriate
Physical setting is too large, cold, or formal
Meeting is too long

Meeting frequency is inappropriate
Leader is authoritative and inflexible
Members are not encouraged
Group is unclear about the purpose
Leader is often unprepared
Participants are put on the spot
Tense moments are ignored
There is a lack of shared leadership
There is a lack of follow-up
Leader is not available before and after the meeting
There is a lack of emphasis on application
There is a lack of transparency or openness during discussions
Members do not know one another
There is a lack of prayer time
Meetings are often canceled
Members have childcare problems
There is no group evaluation
There is a lack of participant diversity
Spiritual smugness exists among some members
Members betray confidences
The meeting has become a social event
Members and the leader have repeated tardiness or absenteeism

How can we avoid these pitfalls? Ask yourself, *What could I do differently to solve this problem? How can I lead members to find a workable solution? How can members help me avoid this pitfall?* You have already taken a first step by identifying them. Being aware of problems, or potential ones, gives the leader an edge. Evaluate each situation and each problem.

Evaluation: How Are We Doing?

Often overlooked, the evaluation step may seem to have nothing to do with how you lead a group, the group's purpose, or the characteristics of your group. However, it is the key to eliminating mistakes, improving effectiveness, and reaching goals, and it should be done before, during, and after every activity.

The "Why" of Evaluation

The goals of an evaluation are:

• to discover the need for and make changes

• to assess the group's progress

• to gather facts and information

• to assess success of the leadership

• to encourage members as they progress toward their goals

• to improve the ministries of the group

To move forward, the group must review regularly the plans for development and the means to implement the plans, and progress must be checked. Evaluation of groups must be deliberate and planned, and should be used to obtain information that will help you make course corrections and group decisions. Information gained in your evaluation can provide guidance for long-range planning, so it is important that you keep good records. For best results, use the same evaluation format at several points in time to help you formulate conclusions and observe progress.

The "When" of Evaluation

When should evaluation take place? It should be an ongoing process, but specific times should be set aside for reporting and updating. Evaluation almost always improves performance, and there are a variety of methods, such as observations, group evaluation activities, and questionnaires. A weekend retreat, with one full day for evaluation and another for brainstorming and planning, is an ideal time to evaluate your group's direction, accomplishments, and purpose.

The "How" of Evaluation

What should be included in an evaluation? These suggestions will help you develop your own evaluation questions.

- How clearly defined are the group's goals?

- Do members and leaders agree on major and minor goals?

- Do members and leaders agree on the way these goals will be reached?

- How would you rate the group's support of activities?

- Do group members have the necessary resources to achieve their purpose?

- How well do members communicate with one another and with the leader?

- How would you rate your own leadership of the group?

- Do members share in the decision-making process?

Each group is unique. The best evaluation for your group is one that recognizes that uniqueness and describes your specific group's strengths and weaknesses in reaching its goals.

Each member should participate in the evaluation, with the understanding that the group shares all observations. The most effective evaluation takes place as the group interacts and shares their comments. As the leader, you can help your members work through any fears and objections they have to evaluations.

Some informal evaluation will take place naturally whether or not you plan it. Sometimes it consists of one or two people sharing their frustrations or grievances after a meeting, and when this happens, the group cannot profit from their private judgments. Only when critical or reflective comments are heard by the whole body can something be done about them. On the other hand, some informal evaluation takes place in the positive feedback you get, in the compliments given, in visible evidences of a healthy group. While informal evaluations aren't completely reliable, they can help you discover areas where you need to do more formal evaluating.

Evaluations

Following are two sample evaluations, one for the group leader and one for the group member. You can adapt them to meet your needs. Use them to evaluate an event or group meeting and your participation and preparation.

Sample Leader Feedback

• Did everyone attend?
• Did relationships get off to a good start and members appear to be bonding?
• Did everyone contribute to the discussions?
• Did any person seem to monopolize the discussion?
• If prayer requests were shared, did you write them down and follow up on them later?
• Did the group agree on goals and objectives?
• Is the group moving toward its goals?
• Did you feel comfortable in your role as leader?

Sample Members' Feedback

Check the statements that describe how you think the group functioned:

___ All members participated.
___ Members listened and were open to what others thought.
___ Members supported one another.
___ We openly worked out differences of opinion.
___ Newcomers to the group felt welcome.
___ We had enough time for agenda items and used the time wisely.
___ We accomplished our task.
___ Our group has activities outside our meetings.
___ We invite others to our group.

Group Assessment Activities

Emily Morrison in her book Leadership Skills suggests this activity as a way to clarify group expectations. You might find it useful as you provide evaluative opportunities for your group.

Ahead of time prepare a handout sheet for each group member.

Step 1: Name some of the things you hope your group accomplishes this year.

What do you think the group should expect of its members?

What abilities or services do you think you can give to the group?

Step 2: Divide your group into pairs and allow time for each to share their answers.

Step 3: Change partners and repeat Step 2.

Step 4: Regroup and discuss the responses.

Step 5: Compile a list of the group's expectations from the responses they've made.

Step 6: Develop ideas for ways to implement the voiced expectations.

Must All Good Things Come to an End?

This final phase of group life—ending the group—may be the greatest single influence on how people react to future groups, and how leaders develop as well. Successfully completing this phase is key to participants feeling satisfied, involved, and eager to participate again.

During the final phase of the group's life, the leadership should begin to:

• lay groundwork for new groups and new leadership
• lead the group in understanding and dealing with termination
• help group members become aware of the psychology of ending a relationship
• help members focus on the accomplishments of the group
• evaluate and praise accomplishments
• complete administrative tasks

These principles apply to any type of group—a task force at work, a church committee, a women's Bible study group, a support group or a mission group.

Termination of a group requires skilled leadership. It means moving from a democratic to an authoritative leadership style. The leader must help members deal openly and honestly with the positive, and if appropriate, the negative feelings associated with termination. Remember, all individuals have different personal feelings about the end of any relationship.

10 Reasons Why Groups End

Group leader Neal McBride has identified ten common grounds for group termination:

1. The stated length of time expires. This is the ideal reason for disbanding groups that began with a clearly defined time span or purpose for existence.

2. The task is accomplished. Once the task is complete, the group has no purpose for continuing.

3. The group explodes in conflict. Usually this occurs fairly early in a group's life.

4. The group has no covenant or common purpose. Members agree that continuing without a purpose is counter-productive.

5. A conscious decision is made to terminate and remain friends, for whatever reason. Schedule conflicts, members moving out of town, the desire to try something new, or reformation of the group are examples.

6. Ineffective leadership results in the group's ending. Action- and need-oriented groups are less patient with ineffective leaders than process-oriented ones.

7. The group divides to form two new groups. This works well in Bible studies and some other situations.

8. The group has poor administration. Poor handling of issues, such as time, place, frequency, and scheduling, can cause members to give up and stop participating.

9. There is conflict with other programs. If people are forced to choose between attending a group or participating in something else, this may mean the end of the group's life.

10. Members are not compatible. A group may end because interests and needs are too dissimilar or there is simply too great a variance in age and experience.

5 Things to Remember

Since ending a group can be a stressful experience, it should be done carefully. Friendships built in groups can be among the most meaningful many people have, and there are certain things a leader should take into consideration when closing a group.

1. Don't be reluctant to talk about the end. Prepare the group for the last meeting before it arrives. Help members to begin to work through the closure process.

2. Use a flexible last meeting format. The most important thing during the last meeting is making sure people go their separate ways with the greatest amount of comfort and confidence.

3. Have fun and encourage one another. Encourage members to say good things about other group members or share how the group has been helpful for them. Give everyone the chance to share.

4. Plan for a future reunion. If feasible, plan a reunion meeting, so everyone can get together again. Let the members know about other opportunities to get involved in groups.

5. Pray together. Make sure your group takes advantage of what they have built together by making their last prayer time as special as possible.

Where Are We Going?

"We will never be better as a team than we are to each other."
—Unknown

We've taken a brief look at groups and their functions. We've seen what makes them healthy and why we have some pretty sick ones in all of our organizations. We know that effective, skilled leadership is the answer for group conflict, accomplishing goals, fulfilling purpose, and being meaningful in the lives of members.

The question that remains is, *Are you effective in the group setting as a leader? Are you the kind of member every leader wants in her group?* There are many variables in group work—so many, in fact, that one wonders how any group is effective! We know members' backgrounds, age, and experiences all impact the outcome of a group's ability to grow, achieve, and serve.

As we continue to learn to work together toward a common purpose, may we be in agreement with Paul when he talked about the body of Christ: "Just as each of us has one body with many members, and these members do not all have the same function, so in Christ we who are many form one body, and each member belongs to all the others" (Romans 12:4–5).

Chapter Five

5

Conflict Management Essentials

by Shirley Schooley

The story of the conflict between the artist Michelangelo and Pope Julius II over the painting of the ceiling of the Sistine Chapel is an absorbing one. The pope and the artist disagreed heatedly over the new design for the ceiling. The conflict became so intense at one point that Michelangelo destroyed what he had painted, ran away, and became a fugitive. However, the final result, the breathtaking ceiling of the Sistine Chapel, is still regarded as Michelangelo's greatest masterpiece. After Michelangelo returned to Rome, one of Julius's military assistants asked Julius why he had given in to Michelangelo in their disagreement. Julius replied, "I planned a ceiling—Michelangelo has planned a miracle." That "miracle" today still leaves people awestruck and silent. Because there was conflict, we have a miracle of art that has, through four centuries, turned human minds to God.

This story serves as illustration that we can use the conflict that is part of all our lives to enrich and enliven rather than destroy. We can use our knowledge of conflict management to help us repair our fragmented families, groups, and organizations. We can accomplish the extraordinary by learning to live together and work together with acceptance and respect for each other and for each other's differences.

This chapter will define conflict and its sources, the types of conflict, how people deal with it, and the leader's role in managing conflict.

"Is!" "Is Not!"

We've all heard children engaged in an argument asserting that something "Is," to which the other replies, "Is not!" Conflict is like that in many respects. All too often we simplify what it means when it involves more than we realize, both in its source and in its management. So, let's look at some "Conflict is" and "Conflict is not" statements in an effort to clarify the dimensions of conflict.

Conflict is not simply a struggle over opposing ideas or values or claims to status, power, or resources. **Conflict is not** people working against each other. What one wants appears to be incompatible with what another wants; what one gets seemingly must come at the expense of the other. The best that can be accomplished is a compromise where each gives up something in order to receive something else.

Because people have incompatible ideas, **conflict is** something likely to happen in many situations. Whether real or imagined, if we believe important differences exist, we assume also that there will be attempts to prevent, obstruct, interfere, injure, or intervene with the desired outcome.

The definition of **conflict is** composed of the following ideas:

1. an assumed incompatibility of ideas or values;
2. a struggle over status, power, or resources;
3. a goal of preventing, obstructing, interfering, injuring, or in some way making it less likely that other persons or groups will accomplish their goals.

Conflict is more often a sign of interdependence, of a need to work together in some way, rather than a sign of competitive, incompatible goals. People with similar interests are often in conflict as they express different views about the best way to do such things as complete tasks, divide work, or distribute the rewards of their joint efforts.

Conflict is not just interpersonal differences. Much of what shapes conflict and starts it in the first place has to do with factors that are beyond the interaction of individual personalities. Some conflict may be caused by the structure of an organization or as a result of the nature of assigned tasks and the natural differences of individuals.

Conflict is not always a destructive and imposing barrier we would be better off without. Wishing we could live without conflicts or avoid discussing them is the real barrier. It **is not** an evil to be avoided. **Conflict is** often a painful experience. This is how the argument goes: "Pain is bad. Conflict is painful. Therefore, conflict must be bad also." While conflict may be bad for us, it can also be good, making this statement seem contradictory.

Conflict is not something that always destroys. What does destroy are the harmful ways of handling conflicts, resulting in lost confidence and effectiveness. **Conflict is** sometimes camouflaged, and dissenting views are suppressed so the organization can appear to be perfect. **Conflict is** seen as unnatural or inappropriate. While we may strive for a perfect organization, one that is free from conflict, if we achieve that, it is doomed to failure because it will be an inflexible one, unable to cope with changes. It will lack the capacity for growth and progress. **Conflict is** beneficial because it can prevent stagnation, stimulate our interest and curiosity, and be the channel through which problems can be aired and solutions found.

Defining Conflict

We have seen what conflict is and what it is not—what then is a workable definition that we can use to help us understand the reasons behind conflict and how we as leaders can be effective in managing it? A useful definition for us is that conflict involves incompatible behaviors. One person is interfering, disrupting, or in some other way making another person's actions less effective. While this different way of viewing conflict may seem minor, it has very real, practical implications.

To resolve something is to settle it. To resolve conflict is to bring it to an end. The term *conflict resolution* reflects the attitude that conflict is something that can be and ought to be settled. Sometimes, however, conflict resolution is just not possible and, in some circumstances, may not be desirable.

For example, suppose Debra and Margaret, co-chairs of a church subcommittee, have serious differences over the content of their report. Each is committed to her position. We know in the end they need to come to some agreement, but the conflict can produce benefits. Margaret will be extra careful as she drafts the report and documents her ideas. Debra will be extra critical as she reads what Margaret writes. The best they might hope for is to manage the conflict. They may never resolve it. However, resolving it might not be desirable at all, for the result of this conflict could be a better report.

We will use the term *conflict management* to refer to handling or dealing with conflict. This term does not imply that conflict necessarily ought to be brought to a swift conclusion. It also does not say that conflict is either good or bad. To suggest that conflict must be resolved quickly denies that it might be good and implies that it would be bad. A more sensible approach is that conflict has the possibility of being either good or bad for individuals or groups.

Do not let the use of the term *conflict management* confuse you. The word *management* implies control of the situation, but it is often clear that we cannot really control anything. I like the way Speed Leas, in his book *Leadership and Conflict* (now out of print), uses the word. He suggests we think of management as when we say, "I haven't figured that out yet, but I'll manage somehow." In this context, *manage* means to get along, make out, or muddle through. Sometimes "muddling through" is the best we can do in the particular situation.

Managing conflict is an essential life skill. Well-managed conflict contributes to the improvement of personal relationships, to the health of our families, to the effectiveness of our churches, and to the productivity of organizations for which we work. In addition, managing conflict well can increase our own feelings of competence. It is a vital skill for those who lead as well as those who follow.

Many organizations, particularly those in the church, have *norms* that discourage any conflict. Norms are the unwritten rules that have sanctions or punishment associated with them and that people live by in order to function as members of a group. If someone fails to abide by the norms of the group, that person will be punished in some way because of the misconduct.

Sometimes a norm means that strong action will be taken to guarantee that no apparent conflict occurs within the organization. When it does occur, those who cause it must either leave or conform. This norm does exist in many groups, particularly volunteer groups, and can become a serious problem for them.

Neither the view that conflict is undesirable because it disrupts the organization, nor the opposing view that considers conflict essential to the effective functioning of every organization is absolutely accurate. Some conflict disrupts our organizations, while other conflict is beneficial. Discriminating between the two kinds, however, is no simple task.

Using conflict in the best interests of the organization requires a thorough understanding of the conflict and the ability to manage it in a way that will allow us to benefit from its positive aspects. Skillfully managed conflict has a good chance of being functional for the organization, while poorly managed conflict may tear the organization apart.

Two Questions

What does the Bible say about conflict? Interestingly, the Bible does not condemn conflict. It seems to say that conflict is at times inevitable, but it does not have to be a sin. Christians do not have to agree on every issue or subject. Each of us has been created in the image of God. We do not have to make everyone think like us. Properly managed conflict can even strengthen us. We are stretched as we deal with conflict. Sometimes God may reveal what He wants us to be as we are in the midst of conflict.

The Book of Proverbs has a lot to say about how believers are to guard their words and work through conflict as it arises. Look up the following verses in Proverbs and paraphrase some of them to imprint them on your memory.

Proverbs 10:19

Proverbs 12:16

Proverbs 15:1

Proverbs 15:18

Proverbs 16:32

Proverbs 18:13

Proverbs 20:3

Proverbs 21:29

Proverbs 26:21

Proverbs 29:11

Are there any benefits of conflict? Whether conflict is bad or good may depend in part on how skillfully it is managed. The belief that conflict must be resolved or controlled is consistent with the view that conflict is inherently bad. Resolution and control are inappropriate reactions for much conflict, and some conflict should even be encouraged and used to help the organization reach its goals.

Too often we have learned inappropriate ways of dealing with conflict and, as a result, have been left frustrated and unprepared to deal with our personal or family conflicts or those in other areas. The problem is not the existence of conflict but the difficulty that people or organizations have in managing conflict constructively. When managed poorly, conflict can become destructive. Properly managed, it can be at the root of personal and social change. Conflict, then, may be seen as a natural occurrence, something to be expected and not to be eliminated or avoided.

Benefit: Controversy is often necessary if people are to feel committed to decisions. When discussion is used to air different opinions and ideas, people are likely to feel satisfied and believe they have benefited from the discussion. They enjoy the excitement, feel stirred by the challenges of the conflict, and become committed to the new agreements or positions. When the position is different from their own, they better understand why the adopted position is superior to their original one.

Benefit: People disclose previously hidden information, challenge their own and others' assumptions, dig into issues, and, as a consequence, understand the problem more thoroughly. The diverse opinions that create conflict are needed to help us better solve problems. **Note:** You as a leader may need to take actions that will ensure that members deal with important issues they may be burying.

Benefit: Conflict can become the medium by which problems are recognized and solved.

Benefit: Managing conflict can help us build healthy, productive relationships. People realize that others are not as arrogant or as vulnerable as previously assumed and recognize their ability to work together to deal with their differences.

Benefit: Conflict brings attention to the existence of a problem that might otherwise be ignored or overlooked. For example, the women's rights and civil rights movements and their resulting conflict brought important problems into the open in American society.

Benefit: Conflict can unify a group, causing the members to set aside destructive or counterproductive disagreements while they attend to the new conflict. Conflict, therefore, can be a motivating force for individuals and for groups and can help create group cohesion and commitment.

Benefit: Conflict can sharpen the issues of a problem situation. We may not realize what our own needs and purposes are until we have to describe and defend them as a result of some conflict. We find we must study it and learn about it in more depth than we had, and as a result conflict can be educational for all involved.

Benefit: The ideas and logic of others can cause us to question whether our original position is as useful and sensible as assumed. We are motivated to search for new information, strengthening our understanding of the situation.

Benefit: We are likely to become more open-minded and knowledgeable about the issue and, if appropriate, change our minds. When we have approached the issue from several perspectives and have not stayed rigidly fixed to our original idea, we are more likely to have a decision that is a good one.

Benefit: Well-managed conflict can strengthen both our personal and our professional relationships. As we confront, rather than avoid conflict, we add honesty and zest to all of our relationships.

Put Another Way . . .

Conflict can bring about:

- *Problem awareness*. Discussing frustrations identifies poor quality, injustices, or other barriers to effectiveness.

• *Improved solutions.* Debating opposing views forces us to dig into issues, to search for information and insight, and to integrate ideas, creating workable solutions.

• *Organizational change.* Conflict often creates changes in procedures, assignments, and structures that are outmoded.

• *Personal development.* Confronting conflicts teaches us how our style affects others and reveals the competencies we need to develop.

• *Knowledge and creativity.* Elaboration and listening help us retain ideas and understand their implications. We become more creative as we explore alternatives and integrate different points of view.

• *Awareness.* Knowing what people are willing to fight about keeps us in touch with each other.

• *Self-acceptance.* Expressing frustrations and important feelings helps us accept and value ourselves, in turn building our self-esteem.

• *Psychological maturity.* Addressing conflicts encourages us to consider the perspectives of others and become less concerned about our own.

• *Morale.* Discussion and problem solving help us release our tensions and stress, making our relationships stronger and more open.

• *Challenge and fun.* The stimulation and involvement of conflict can be enjoyable, even a welcome break from monotony.

There is excitement, then, in the idea that conflict is not only a natural part of our lives, but also can teach us valuable lessons about ourselves and about others. As we struggle, we learn how to solve problems and reach useful agreements, and our relationships become stronger, more productive, and enjoyable. We begin to be more confident of our ability to deal with conflict in the future. As we learn that conflict can be managed and does not have to destroy, we can face opposing issues and have less need to impose our way on others.

"We should always keep a corner
of our heads open and free, that
we may make room for the
opinions of our friends.""
—Joubert

Conflict Comes in Many Colors

If we are to accomplish tasks in our organizations or sustain
important relationships, we must learn to cope effectively with
conflict. Conflict is very much a part of our daily lives.

As leaders, we are responsible for coordinating and integrat-
ing the work of many different people. This blending of the
energies and personalities of members of our organization,
employees of our company, or persons in our family will naturally result in conflict. In well-managed conflict, though, we
highlight potential difficulties, encourage new solutions, and

ensure the continued commitment and interest of others. Someone has said, "If two people always agree, one of them is unnecessary." Alan Randolph and Barry Posner expressed this idea more clearly in their book, *Getting the Job Done* (now out of print): "Conflicts are born out of caring. People do not fight about issues they don't care about."

Conflict, then, evolves naturally from our relationships and situations, as well as from our personalities. Knowing the source of a conflict may help you to isolate its cause and deal more effectively with it. Therefore, we will look at several ways of categorizing conflict.

The Color Green—
"Ideas" as a Source of Conflict

Just as we think of green representing new growth in the spring, it could be connected to the presenting and testing of new ideas. New ideas are not always well received (remember how people laughed at inventions such as the telephone, television, and airplanes?). Idea conflict may sometimes focus on the values that underlie the preference individuals have for a particular idea.

Conflict related to values is generally more intense and prolonged than conflict related simply to ideas. Value conflict revolves around goals and means. If your group is having trouble making a decision, ask members if they agree on basic goals. Often members submit one proposal after another and are rejected each time. This is usually a sign of a goal problem.

Sometimes the problem is a basic disagreement about how the group is proceeding. Your task force at work may be in conflict not over the newly proposed idea for efficiency but over how it will be implemented. If you lead a support group for young women and there is conflict over the purpose of the group, you have value concerns that must be resolved before a group can function effectively.

The Color Gold—
"Status" as a Source of Conflict

Gold denotes special standing, whether it's an Oscar, a gold star for 100% on a spelling test, or a wedding band signifying a marriage vow. It is almost synonymous with status. *Status* refers to the position of a member in a group hierarchy, a ranking members on the basis of each person's perceived importance. Status consensus is agreement on where members fit in the hierarchy. Dissatisfaction with one's status will generally lead to tension and conflict. Members weigh such things as each member's contribution, personality, and so forth, and come to some sense of their importance to the group. Conflict can occur as the group members work through the process of establishing a status hierarchy.

A *hidden agenda* refers to goals or objectives that a member may have—and chooses not to reveal—that differ from those of the group. Often these are status conflicts masquerading as an idea conflict. For example, June may want to be more influential, so she challenges every idea proposed by the group leader or members in order to seem influential. As a leader, look at what June does not say; watch for negative behavior. Listen for judgmental statements to see if she is positive about anything. Are only her ideas worthwhile? Does she couch her antagonism toward you as a leader under the guise of "being helpful" or "I have a suggestion . . ."?

Watch also the way the persons involved are interacting. Two high contributors competing for status will sometimes attack each other. A challenger will direct attacks at the person with the higher status, many times making a pretense at humor or with statements that attempt to negate what she really means.

The Color Red—
"Need For Power" as a Source of Conflict

Do you have a red power suit that you wear for important meetings or events? The color red makes many feel powerful.

Power, closely related to status, is the perceived influence one person has over another. Because power is the ability to influence others, some use it for selfish purposes while others use it in a responsible way to accomplish important objectives. Conflict can arise when members think a person is using power inappropriately.

For example, if Bobbie comes to your Bible study group completely unprepared, conflict (or at the very least, tension) will arise because group members feel she should not lead if she does not prepare. Bobbie has disregarded the power that has been entrusted to her. Others in her position may take the power they have as leader and misuse it when they dictate all curriculum materials and control all discussion. These examples are important sources of conflict in interpersonal and group relationships.

Types of Conflict

Different types of conflict produce different results.

One type of conflict involves opposition related to ideas or issues. The focus is on the content—the ideas. Suppose the facilitator of your group calls the members together to discuss whether you should meet once a week or once every other week. Carla thinks the group should meet every week; Joy believes every other week is adequate.

This conflict can arise from disagreements over facts (what really happened or will happen), over the value or significance of the situation itself, over policies and procedures, over the allocation of rewards, over the course of action to take, or over the goals or purposes of the group or organization and the best methods for attaining those goals or purposes. It reveals an intellectual opposition of group members to the content of ideas or issues important to the group task.

Another type of conflict involves the emotions of anger, mistrust, fear, and resentment and includes personality clashes. Such conflict does not ordinarily stem from a disagreement based on opinions or beliefs, but from a struggle based on selfish or personal issues. It is rooted in emotional and interpersonal relations. Consider the situation mentioned earlier.

Carla: "Joy, you want to meet only once every two weeks because it would be more convenient for you. You know we need to meet more than that. I really resent your attitude about this."

Joy: "I can't imagine that you would say anything like that. Who do you think you are to be able to read my mind and tell me what I think? You're dead wrong about all of this."

Joy and Carla's conflict is the type that is often characterized by clashes over self-oriented or personal needs. Perhaps they both have a need to dominate. Thus, the focus is on interpersonal and social issues rather than value and idea issues. Personal conflicts can lead to defensiveness and counterproductive behavior.

A group that experiences value/idea conflict solves its conflict largely through the use of facts and efficient problem solving. Such groups are aided by warm and friendly interpersonal relationships. Joy and Carla might have solved their conflict by presenting their reasons for wanting different schedules for meetings.

Groups experiencing emotional and interpersonal conflict may seem to handle it by avoiding meeting the issue head on. Withdrawal in this case reduces the likelihood that the members of the group will come to agreement. In this example, either Carla or Joy may withdraw from the conflict. A word of warning is appropriate here. Such unresolved conflicts often deteriorate into emotional conflict.

The "Pieces and Parts" of Conflict

Helpful or *constructive conflict* is a means to an end. Because it offers individuals and groups a chance to identify and solve problems, it can bring positive benefits and further the group's progress toward its goal. *Conflict that is destructive*, however, is an end in itself and is not directly associated with any goal. For example, in the workplace we may find a situation where one worker may go on strike to gain higher wages and better working conditions. Another worker may engage in the same strike because of some hatred of the employer.

The *intensity of the conflict* is related to several variables. The more important and attractive the individual goals, the more intense the conflict is likely to be. Suppose I am the leader of a group. If I know the group is about to make a decision that will be very difficult to implement, and if I think the decision will cause me a great deal of grief, I will fight hard to defeat the proposal.

The *relative attractiveness* of the options also affects the intensity of the conflict. If the group perceives two ideas to be equally attractive, there is likely to be great conflict, especially if the members also see the alternatives as being important. Conflict of this type is called *approach-approach conflict.* On an individual basis, we all experience this when we stand in front of the movie theater trying to decide between two movies, both of which we want to see. On a more significant level, we may be job hunting and suddenly find ourselves offered two equally good jobs. In situations when one alternative seems somewhat more attractive than the other, there is less conflict.

A group may find that the ideas it is considering have both attractive and unattractive features. A solution to a parking problem at church might provide more space for people to park but cause them to walk much farther. Such a situation produces *approach-avoidance conflict.*

A less common, but still important situation is the one where we must choose between two negative and equally unattractive alternatives—*avoidance-avoidance conflict.*

Finally, the *number of ideas* to consider may affect the conflict. The group that sees several possible alternatives as equally attractive and sees its decision as an important one may experience very intense conflict. Members want to make the best decision, but they are likely to have trouble sorting through the many possible alternatives.

Three Stages of Conflict

Conflict management may depend on recognizing how far along the parties are in a particular conflict. In general, conflicts seem to go through three major stages.

1. Latent conflicts are characterized by the recognition of some underlying tensions. People have not felt the need to take sides yet; the conflict is not highly polarized. At this stage, some, but not all, participants begin to be aware of the coming conflict.

2. Emerging conflict is when all parties involved acknowledge that a disagreement or dispute exists. At this stage, there is potential for the conflict to escalate. People sense that tension is building in all potential participants.

3. Manifest conflict is the stage of open, ongoing conflict. The people involved may have already begun to seek ways to resolve or deal with the conflict—negotiation, bargaining, or intervention by a third party.

Role Conflicts

Role conflict occurs when one person or group of persons in a role is unable to respond to or meet the expectations of others. All of us fill many roles each day, some formal, some informal. Likewise, some are related to our jobs or other outside organizations, while some are related to our marriages, children, and homes. For example, a professional accountant who is also a wife and mother, and her husband, who is also an engineer and father, will experience role conflict when they must deal with a sick child on the same day they both have mandatory meetings at work.

We can identify five basic types of role conflicts.

1. Intrasender role conflict occurs when one person sends a role holder inconsistent expectations. For example, a wife may expect her husband to earn a lot of money and be successful on the job while still spending a lot of time with the family. Likewise, husbands often want a wife to help earn part of the family income but still do all the things we associate with a traditional full-time homemaker.

2. Intersender role conflict occurs when different persons with whom the role holder interacts have different expectations of her. Her boss may expect her to work late when needed, while her children want her home early each evening. At work, a role holder may have a superior who expects her to keep very close watch on her subordinates, while her subordinates want more freedom to do their work in the way they see best.

3. Person-role conflict occurs when the values and needs of the role holder conflict with the expectations of others. For example, we may be expected to do something at work that we consider unethical.

4. Interrole conflict occurs when the expectations associated with different roles a person holds come into conflict. A working mother who has a sick child feels she is expected to perform her job at work and be at home to care for her sick child at the same time.

5. Role overload conflict is a situation where the expectations sent to the role holder are compatible, but there is not enough time to perform all the expected activities. Leaders may inadvertently cause this type of conflict when they simply hand out task assignments without understanding the stress they may be causing members.

Role conflict may also arise from the structure of the organization. For example, a group facilitator or leader may see her role as one of developing policy and strategy rather than actually doing the work, while the other officers or the members may expect the president to do some of the work herself.

```
┌─────────────────────────────────────────────┐
│ ┌─────────────────────────────────────────┐ │
│ │          Role Conflicts in Your Life     │ │
│ │  Do you ever send inconsistent messages  │ │
│ │  to your children? Cite an example.      │ │
│ │                                          │ │
│ │                                          │ │
│ │  Have you ever experienced a work        │ │
│ │  situation where there was a conflict    │ │
│ │  with another area of your life?         │ │
│ │                                          │ │
│ │                                          │ │
│ │  Can you think of a time when you had a  │ │
│ │  person-role conflict over an ethical    │ │
│ │  issue at work?                          │ │
│ │                                          │ │
│ └─────────────────────────────────────────┘ │
└─────────────────────────────────────────────┘
```

Hazards, Hazards Everywhere!

Conflict can be analyzed in terms of whether it is fundamental or superficial, short-term or long-term. For example, we can imagine a conflict that is long lasting or even permanent between two groups in an organization. Such a long-standing conflict, resulting perhaps from a different view of what the goals of the organization should be, will be more difficult to resolve than a minor disagreement concerning methods for meeting an agreed-upon goal.

Sometimes procedures for doing work may be unclear, poorly carried out, or contradictory, thus creating opportunities for conflict. These difficulties can usually be worked out rather easily. The trick is to identify that you have a procedural problem and do something about it. If you are in the midst of conflict, see if procedures are part of the problem.

Conflicts over goals are usually more significant and more difficult to resolve than conflicts concerning practical means to achieve those ends. If people feel their self-esteem is at stake or is threatened, or if they feel in danger of losing face, the conflict may not be easily resolved. Personality clashes, therefore, can sometimes be difficult to resolve. Of course, when conflict occurs in a group, it usually comes from more than one source.

Here is a list of sources of conflict that seem to exist naturally when a group is working on a project. Conflicts typically arise over the following seven points of contention.

1. Project priorities: Group members may differ over the proper sequencing of activities and tasks. *Has anyone ever questioned your leadership about determining project priorities? What did you do?*

2. Administrative procedures: How will responsibilities be assigned? What support will be given to the accomplishing of those assignments? *As a leader, have you made inappropriate assignments?*

3. Technical opinions: When the task to be accomplished is not a routine one, opinions may differ widely on the best way to accomplish the task. *Name an instance when you disagreed with how a project was carried out.*

4. Staffing and resource allocations: How will tasks be assigned? For example, one group member may complain that she gets all the "grunt work" while another gets the easier, more visible assignments. *Think of a time when you were unhappy because you were given the hardest assignment.*

5. Costs and budgets: Money almost always becomes a point of contention in any task to be accomplished. If you have built or remodeled a home, been responsible for a church or community project, or led a task force at work, you have probably faced this type of conflict. *How have you as a leader handled conflict over costs and budgets?*

6. Schedules: Time is another source of tension. A first question for many of us when facing a task, either simple or complex, is "How much time will it take?" *How does this kind of conflict affect you as a leader?*

7. Interpersonal and personality clashes: Conflict often will arise over ego-centered issues like status, power, control, self-esteem, and friendships. *Write a brief description of a personality clash that happened and which you had to address as a leader.*

Ways People Deal With Conflict

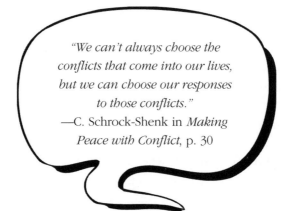

> "We can't always choose the
> conflicts that come into our lives,
> but we can choose our responses
> to those conflicts."
> —C. Schrock-Shenk in *Making
> Peace with Conflict*, p. 30

People generally use a number of strategies to manage conflict. We can classify these strategies according to their likely outcomes: win-lose, lose-lose, lose-win, and win-win. You could probably compose such a list yourself by recalling your experiences with conflict. Your list might include some of the strategies described here.

Win-Lose Strategy

When power is used to force the other person to accept a position, each party tries to figure out how to get the upper hand, thereby causing one person to lose. A win-lose outcome occurs when one party in the conflict achieves his or her goal when the other loses. A leader using this style might say, "As leader, I'll settle the issue. We will . . ."

Generally, each side sees the conflict only from its own point of view, rather than from a viewpoint that considers mutual needs. Although this style might be appropriate, if the two individuals or groups involved need to continue to work together, then eventually the damaging effects of the win-lose orientation will create difficulties. If we win a conflict with a colleague, for example, she may not be willing to be supportive of us in the future when her support may be critical. The conflict is often not really resolved but continues, perhaps below the surface. The win-lose approach is a tempting one when you have more power than the other person.

When quick decisions and actions are vital or when you are absolutely sure you are correct, this style might be the most appropriate one for us to use. You may be aware of information not available to others in the group.

Lose-Lose Strategy—Avoidance

A lose-lose outcome occurs if, as a result of a conflict-management episode, both parties lose or fail to achieve all or part of their goals. A typical behavior used by a leader choosing this strategy might be: "Let's not talk about that today. I'd rather move on to something else." Often a leader may feel that she may not have the skills and confidence needed to confront conflict successfully. She may believe that avoiding the situation and requiring others to do likewise is the safest option. When we retreat from a conflict situation, we usually satisfy neither our own nor the other person's concern.

We may also be tempted to use this strategy when we know we cannot win, but we hope that by ignoring the problem the other side will also be unable to win. Of course, in this type of situation the conflict usually does not go away, but becomes even more unmanageable.

Recently I attended a meeting where one of the participants asked an important question that needed to be answered. However, it was one with no easy answer and one that would raise many underlying issues. Conflict over the answer was almost assured. The leader's response was: "We have too many items on the agenda to discuss that today!" If it is not answered soon, the organization may soon find itself facing issues that will make its long-term survival difficult.

A positive use of the avoiding strategy would be when the leader decides that the time is not right for escalating the conflict or that this problem will resolve itself over time. For example, two individuals in the group may have difficulty working together, but the leader is aware that one of them is moving soon. Intervention may create even more difficulty rather than solve the problem.

Several years ago, I had a good friend and colleague who lived in my neighborhood. She was in the midst of raising teenage children and was dealing with the many conflicts most parents of teenagers experience. I had seen her handle conflict at work and knew she was not one to avoid confrontation. However, she was smart enough to know that immediate confrontation was not always the best strategy.

Therefore, when she found herself in the midst of conflict with one of her children, she would walk around the block several times, often stopping by my house for a few minutes. Then, in a calmer moment, she would go back to cope with the situation. Such a strategy not only improved her mental well-being but her physical well-being as well. Staying away from a conflict situation until tempers have cooled is not avoiding the conflict, but rather is a specific strategy for dealing with it.

Lose-Lose Strategy—Compromise

In a compromise strategy, each person hopes to gain a little and give a little. In this strategy, nobody wins all; everyone loses something. Members on a finance committee using this strategy might make a decision such as: "It looks as if Frances would like to give the Missions Committee $1,000. Cindy would like to give the Family Program the $1,000. Let's give each $500."

The decision to share the "pie" rather than have the whole thing is often the way we approach many small conflicts we have in our lives. We avoid arguing continually over minor issues by agreeing that our spouse will choose the television show at 7:00 and we will choose at 8:00, or by letting the other driver cut in even when we have the right-of-way. Some things in both our personal lives and our professional lives are simply too insignificant to warrant an investment in conflict.

Lose-Win Strategy

What we lose in order to accommodate the other side, they win. Accommodating often is an attempt to appease the other side, perhaps because we believe they are too powerful for us to resist. On the other hand, we may not wish to jeopardize our relationship by holding out in a conflict.

We may accommodate the other side if we see some long-range benefit from the gains they might make. If, for example, a customer stays with us as a result of our giving in one time, they may be in a position to become even better customers in the future. In many relationships, however, this strategy results in repressed anger on the part of the one who continually loses, which will eventually affect the quality of the relationship.

Win-Win Strategy

The win-win strategy emphasizes directing your energies toward confronting and defeating the problem, not the other person. An open exchange of information is encouraged, and those involved try to reach a solution that meets the needs of all concerned.

This is a good strategy to use when future relationships and cooperation are important and compromise is not appropriate. Those taking a win-win approach do not assume that what one side wins the other side must lose. When we use this approach, we are assuming that the conflict results from a problem that both sides, working together, can solve. Problem solvers try to understand the conflict from the other's point of view, searching for solutions that meet everyone's needs.

Although this approach seems to fit our ideas of how Christians might deal with conflict, it is not always possible to use this strategy. In situations where incompatible goals and values are at stake, or if those involved do not have the motivation or the ability to deal with their conflicts, it will not be successful.

Get Me Outta Here!
Dealing with Difficult People

If you find yourself in a current conflict situation involving a difficult person, you may want to remove yourself, if you can! Of course, realistically, we cannot always run. If this person is our boss, a family member, or other significant individual in our lives, we may have to find another job, move away, or otherwise determine how to minimize that person's impact on our lives.

Sandra Crowe in *Since Strangling Isn't an Option* has a great deal of insight into dealing with the difficult persons all of us encounter in leadership positions and in everyday living. Following are several statements you may find helpful in understanding how individuals impact various conflict situations. Can you apply any of them to a current conflict issue with which you are dealing?

"The closer we get to blame, the further we move from solutions." p. 41

"Real change is not without some discomfort. Facing difficult people is tough, but not dealing with them will lead to greater problems in the long run." p. 68

"Conflict occurs in relationships. How we handle the conflict is a reflection of our commitment to the relationship." p.78

"Knowing what motivates people can help you understand behavior, and understanding gives you the opportunity to change it." p. 107

"Devote 20 percent of the time to the problem, and 80 percent to

the solution." p. 123

"Understanding the difficult person reduces your irritation level, makes you feel better, and puts you in a better state to deal with those situations when they arise." p. 171

Remember . . .

- The response others make to our attempts to manage conflict may cause us to change our strategy.
- Carefully evaluate any situation and make a judgment about what will work for you.
- What works well in one situation may be entirely wrong for another.
- Our personalities will determine how we are most likely to respond to conflict.
- It is important to realize that we will avoid some conflicts, choose to compromise in others, and be determined to win in others.
- We have to be flexible enough to use the approach most suitable to the situation.
- The history of the conflict, our relationship to the parties involved, and the situation will all influence our choice of conflict strategies.

Ten Most Common Irrational Ideas

Review Albert Ellis's list to see if they are similar to those you have when in a conflict situation. Rewrite three of them so they reflect rational rather than irrational ideas.

1. It is a dire necessity for an adult to be loved or approved by almost everyone for virtually everything she or he does.

2. One should be thoroughly competent, adequate, and achieving in all possible respects.

3. Certain people are bad, wicked, or villainous and they should be severely blamed and punished for their sins.

4. It is terrible, horrible, and catastrophic when things are not going the way one would like them to go.

5. Human unhappiness is externally caused and people have little or no ability to control their sorrows or rid themselves of their negative feelings.

6. If something is or may be dangerous or fearsome, one should be terribly occupied with and upset about it.

7. It is easier to avoid facing many life difficulties and self-responsibilities than to undertake more rewarding forms of self-discipline.

8. The past is all-important, and because something once strongly affected one's life, it should indefinitely do so.

9. People and things should be different from the way they are, and it is catastrophic if perfect solutions to the grim realities of life are not immediately found.

10. Maximum human happiness can be achieved by inertia and inaction or by passively and uncommittedly enjoying oneself.

From Blame to Discovery:
The Leader and Conflict

"Fix it long before it breaks!"
—H.N. Malony in *Win-Win Relationships* p. 134

I have a good friend who is an administrator for a firm of professionals. One evening at a party we were both attending, someone asked him what he did. He replied, "I herd cats."

After the expected laughter had died away, he elaborated on his statement. "Trying to keep that group all going in the same direction is a real challenge. Some days I wonder how we get anything accomplished."

Does that sound familiar to you? The task of a leader, whether as a manager of professionals, a leader of volunteers, or any other leadership role, requires a commitment to stay the course regardless of the frustrations that may come. Never is this so true as when we try to help our group manage conflict constructively. We may often feel like the person who said, "For every problem, there is a solution that is simple, direct, and wrong."

Success in leadership comes not from our ability to manage when things are going well, but from the way we handle adversity and the challenge brought to our leadership skills by conflict. As a leader, it is your responsibility to move members past the conflicts that would tear them apart, toward a unity of spirit as they pursue worthy goals.

Before beginning to help your group manage conflict, be sure you are starting from a basis of absolute integrity. Integrity that comes from self-knowledge, candor, and maturity is a basic ingredient of leadership. Integrity forms the basis for others to trust us. It then must be combined with sensitivity, tact, compassion, diplomacy, and a genuine caring for others. You must come to the arena of conflict with a servant heart. Then, and only then, are you ready to lead others into and through conflict.

As you lead a group in managing conflict, consider the following ideas:

1. Point those in conflict toward common goals.

At times, we may be able to identify a common goal that will overshadow the opposing interests of those in conflict and will make them willing to work together toward this goal. We put the emphasis on those things that tie us together rather than those things that are pulling us apart. Keep in mind what you have in common, not what you disagree about.

2. Use problem solving.

Problem solving is characterized by an open and trusting exchange of viewpoints. In this approach, we recognize that we can disagree with someone and still be able to work with her or remain her friend. Ask such fundamental questions as: *Who is in conflict? Who can resolve the conflict? What are the barriers to managing the conflict? What was the triggering event that started the conflict? Is all the information available? Has all available information been examined?* Defining the conflict in specific terms gives members a place to start in discussing the problem.

Everyone should be asked to give as much relevant information as they have. Then encourage the group to search for new information that might shed helpful light on the subject. Create alternative solutions, and do not assume your first solution is best.

3. Focus on the issues, not personalities.

Keep your focus on helping people feel accepted and valued even when others criticize their ideas. Do not attempt to assign blame, because blaming behavior leads to defensiveness, which in turn leads to a more rigid position and poor communication. Always remember that the people you blame are quite likely to blame you back! Simply telling people to cooperate is not particularly helpful. After all, if it were so simple, we would not have conflict in the first place!

4. Keep everyone informed about what is happening.

The more information that is shared, the more people are informed, and the less threatening the experience. Servant leadership is characterized by openness, by an ability to listen, and by engaging people directly in the issues.

5. Share rewards for success; share responsibility for failure.

At the heart of the learning organization is the ability to evaluate what has happened and learn from it. Analyze your experiences, examine them, reflect on them, and struggle to

understand them. Remember that it is acceptable to make mistakes as long as you make them in good conscience while
doing the best you can.

Questions for Reflection

Which statements describe how you normally respond
to conflict?

- I am likely to give up something in order to get
something.
- I do whatever is necessary to avoid arguments and
tension.
- I am usually firm about pursuing my goals or
objectives.
- I normally ask others for help in working out a
solution to a problem.
- I let others take the responsibility for solving
problems.
- I favor a direct discussion of disagreements.

What do your answers reveal to you

Let's Work This Out

Healthy groups develop a norm that goes something like this:
If you have a disagreement with another member, tell that person what is bothering you; if you have a disagreement with
the group, share your opinions with the group. Norms that
discourage direct sharing of differences between members and
the group make successful conflict management almost
impossible to accomplish.

Leaders discourage direct sharing of differences when they . . .

1. Tell group members they are in danger of losing something and must present a united front.

2. Tell those group members who disagree with others in the group that they are not team players and need to cooperate more.

3. Tell group members that "I know you will do the 'right thing.'"

4. Hold controversial agenda items until the end of the meeting when those in opposition may have left or are tired and ready to leave.

What's a Leader to Do?

When we serve as leader of a group, we need to **remind the group** that cooperation and conflict are not opposites and the choice is not an either/or situation. People who work together in a trusting relationship have the confidence that others will respond and listen with open minds to their opinions.

Remind group members that they can feel free to state and explain their ideas. As the group deals openly with conflict, they repeat and add new information, present additional ideas, and elaborate on their positions. Through this process, better decisions are made and the group learns that it is possible for a group of people to acknowledge their differences and still love one another.

Remind the group to define its common goals and find ways of achieving them. This is essential in conflict management. Until members can see what is dividing them, the conflict will remain and may escalate out of control.

Remind yourself that the transforming leader helps group members look beyond what divides them to see the common purpose that provides the glue of unity. The leader empowers the group by helping members find a way to do what they have felt helpless to accomplish by themselves.

Remind yourself also that the size of the group will affect your ability to manage conflict. The larger the group, the more difficult it is to understand the complexities of any problem. You may find it helpful to divide the group into smaller, more manageable groups, as this will help individuals use common sense, bond with each other, and maintain good relationships as they struggle with various issues.

Remind others that learning together provides the support and feedback needed for personal change.

Remind yourself that as the group reaches maturity in terms of its ability to deal constructively with conflict, the members may resist depending on you for guidance. At some stages of the group's life, the leader's support for any idea may generate resistance from those who need to prove themselves by challenging you.

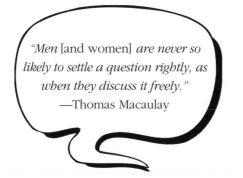

"Men [and women] *are never so likely to settle a question rightly, as when they discuss it freely."*
—Thomas Macaulay

Question for Reflection
Think about your own experience in a recent conflict. Describe how it might have been managed better if people had been able to talk openly about how to manage it.

Is Conflict Natural in Group Life?

Knowing something about typical stages that groups go through can help us realize that much conflict is simply a natural part of people learning to work together. The duration and intensity of these stages will vary from group to group. It helps to know that even when a group starts out working well together, progress is rarely smooth. Although the group generally begins with hope and optimism, boredom, frustration, or impatience may set in as the activities get underway and members realize how much has to be done. Understanding these stages of growth will help you and your group to avoid overreacting to normal conflict.

Stage 1: Forming

When a group is forming, members are "testing the waters" to determine what types of behavior are acceptable. This stage of transition from individual to member status and of testing the leader's guidance may be a difficult time for a leader. When the group is forming, members usually have a mixture of feelings, such as pride in the group and anxiety about the task ahead. During this stage, members define the task, decide how it will be accomplished, and establish ground rules for acceptable behavior.

Lofty, abstract discussions of concepts and issues may cause impatience and questions about their relevance. Problems such as scheduling future meetings, finding a meeting location, and obtaining necessary resources are also part of this stage. Because these distractions get so much of their attention in the beginning, members accomplish little, if anything, that concerns their ultimate goals. This is a perfectly normal, if somewhat frustrating, situation.

Stage 2: Storming

Probably the most difficult stage is storming, when members begin to realize the task is more difficult than they imagined.

They are often attempting to redefine the task, trying to agree on organizational objectives and strategy, and determining their degree of commitment to it. They may experience resistance to approaches that are different from what they have experienced in the past. Leaders must be prepared to deal with group members who may argue among themselves and establish unrealistic goals. These pressures mean there is little energy to spend on progressing toward the goals of the organization. Although this stage is difficult, if a group skips this stage, it may not have looked critically or objectively at all the issues.

Stage 3: Norming

Feelings of cohesiveness develop during the norming stage. New group ground rules (norms) are adopted, and cooperative relationships begin to develop. Conflict is reduced. A group will normally experience a new ability to express criticism constructively and express relief that it seems everything is going to work out.

The leader needs to foster an interest in finding mutually acceptable solutions and a shared responsibility for the group's activities without conflict. As group members begin to work out their differences, they now have more time and energy to spend on the tasks to be done, and some action may occur. Occasionally, a group will not reach this stage, resulting in its disintegration.

Stage 4: Performing

By the fourth stage, members have settled group relationships and expectations. This is the maturity stage for the group as they begin working toward accomplishing their goals. The group's structure, which emerged during the storming stage, now contributes directly to getting things done. At this stage, the leader assists the group to work through problems and become a cohesive unit that gets a lot of work done.

Limping Into the Future

One leadership essential is to become competent in managing both minor conflicts and important conflicts constructively. As we become more effective, we strengthen our relationships with others, improve our sense of individual competence, and gain the ability to reach and lead others.

As a leader, your most important conflict management skill will be your ability to bring people together and persuade them to engage in the process of learning to deal constructively with conflict. Opening up discussion and getting the other person or group committed to talking is the first step, and the most difficult. The idea of talking about conflict may seem strange to you, and may seem even stranger to the one with whom you are in conflict. In fact, he or she may initially mistrust your intentions and require clear evidence that you are committed to finding a better way to manage conflict.

Dean Tjosvold in *Learning to Manage Conflict* (now out of print) said this about managing conflict: "Learning to manage conflict is useful even when others are unwilling to join you. If others refuse to join in your efforts, you will, at the very least, have the satisfaction of knowing that you have been willing to take a risk and attempt to work things out. You can also feel confident that you have done all that can be done."

In Margery Williams' wonderful little book, *The Velveteen Rabbit*, the Skin Horse tells Rabbit that "Real isn't how you are made. It's a thing that happens to you. . . . it doesn't happen to people who break easily, or have sharp edges, or who have to be carefully kept." Like Rabbit, we sometimes wish we could become real without uncomfortable things happening to us.

But life isn't like that. We must struggle, confront, and otherwise engage fully in life if we are to become all that God intended us to be. If in that process we are sometimes bruised

and hurt, we can find comfort in the knowledge that throughout the ages God's people have often been in conflict, even
with God, but have found acceptance from Him.

M. Scott Peck retells the Genesis story of Jacob's struggle
throughout a long night with a stranger sent from God. After
the struggle, the stranger tells Jacob that from that moment on
his name would be Israel, because he struggled with God and
with men, and prevailed. And, to use Peck's wonderful sentence, "Jacob limped off into the future."

So we must go, sometimes bruised, perhaps limping a bit,
into our future, modeling in the midst of our conflict the
forgiving, accepting grace of God.

Additional Reading

Communication Essentials

Carol Kent, *Speak Up With Confidence* (Colorado Springs, CO: NavPress, 1997).

Dr. Tom Nash, *The Christian Communicator's Handbook* (Colorado Springs, CO: Victor, 1995).

Relationship Essentials

Esther Burroughs, *A Garden Path to Mentoring* (Birmingham, AL: New Hope Publishers, 1997).

Edna Ellison, *Friend to Friend* (Birmingham, AL: New Hope Publishers, 2002).

Edna Ellison, *Woman to Woman: Preparing Yourself to Mentor* (Birmingham, AL: New Hope Publishers, 1999).

L.B. Hanks, *Vision, Variety, and Vitality: Teaching Today's Adult Generations* (Nashville, TN: Convention Press, 1996).

Marlene D. LeFever, *Learning Styles: Reaching Everyone God Gave You to Teach* (Colorado Springs, CO: David C. Cook Publishing Company, 2002).

Group Building Essentials

Barbara Joiner, *Yours for the Giving: Spiritual Gifts* (Birmingham, AL: New Hope Publishers, 2004).

James L. Lundy, *TEAMS: Together Each Achieves More Success* (Chicago, IL: Dartnell Corp., 1994).

Joyce Mitchell, *Teams Work! A No-Nonsense Approach to Team Building* (Birmingham, AL: WMU, 2003).

Time Management Essentials

Richard Foster, *Celebration of Discipline* (San Francisco: Harper San Francisco, 1997).

Joanna Weaver, *Having a Mary Heart in a Martha World* (Colorado Springs, CO: WaterBrook Press, 2002).

Stephanie Winston, *The Organized Executive* (New York: Warner Business, 2001).

Conflict Management Essentials

Arthur Paul Boers, *Never Call Them Jerks: Healthy Responses to Difficult Behavior* (The Alban Institute, 1999).

General Leadership Essentials

Emily Morrison, *Leadership Skills: Developing Volunteers for Organizational Success* (New York: Perseus Books Group, 1994).

Samuel D. Rima, *Leading from the Inside Out* (Grand Rapids, MI: Baker Books, 2000).